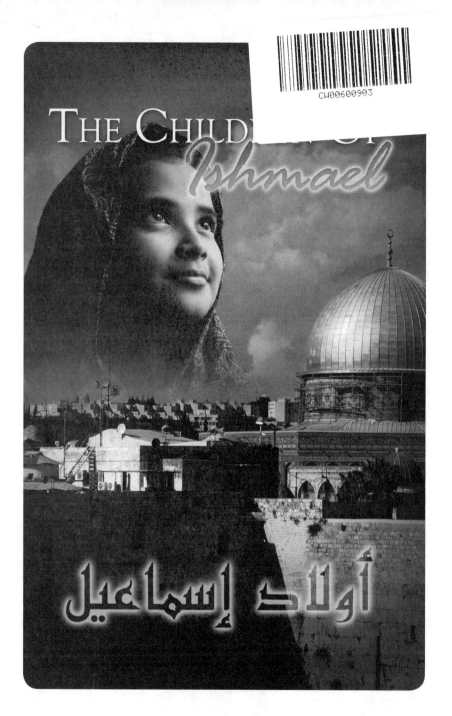

THE CHILDREN OF
Ishmael

أولاد إسماعيل

ANM
publishers

CW00600903

Copyright 2008 by Advancing Native Missions

All rights reserved. Written permission must be
secured from Advancing Native Missions to use or
reproduce any part of this book, except for brief
quotations in critical reviews or articles.

ISBN (13-digits): 978-0-9794929-1-4
ISBN (10-digits): 0-9794929-1-2

Published by Advancing Native Missions
P.O. Box 5303
Charlottesville, VA 22905

Printed in the United States of America

Contents

Introduction

As the prodigal son went back to his father after a time of being lost, going astray, and wandering aimlessly, Ishmael today goes back to the bosom of his father, Abraham, even to the bosom of Christ, who exists before his father, Abraham. He exists before the foundation of the world.

Ishmael goes back to the One who came from heaven and was incarnated for him. Yes, my God and my Savior, you came to preach the Good News to the poor, to bind up the brokenhearted, to proclaim freedom for the captives and release from darkness the prisoners, to bestow on them a crown of beauty instead of ashes, the oil of gladness, instead of mourning, a garment of praise, instead of a spirit of despair.

You came to rebuild the ancient ruins and restore the places long devastated; we will renew the ruined cities that have been devastated for generations, and proclaim freedom, peace, healing, and love. Oh, my God and Savior, you came to save all nations.

We, the children of Ishmael, have lived so many years unaware of you, knowing nothing about you, and many times we not only denied you, but also were hostile to you and fought against you. But your love that is beyond all minds, all imagination, and beyond all enmity found us, guided us, had mercy upon us, and purified us.

Your love, my Savior, brought us back to you as the prodigal to the bosom of his father, as a foundling returns to his mother's bosom, as a drowning person brought back to the ship of rescue.

My God and my Savior, here we are; we sought You and You found us; we asked You and You answered us; we prayed to You and You have heard our prayers. You have loved us first.

Now we have become sons, not slaves; free, not captives. We became righteous instead of being wicked; we became like you in loving the whole nations.

We are the Children of Ishmael, the sons of our father, Abraham, who was called 'the friend of God.' We decided on the next few pages to proclaim to all nations our love, admiration, submission and loyalty to You. We are the branches and You are the vine; we are the bride and You are the groom; we are your city and You are our God, Savior and King.

Yours,

The Children of Ishmael

BEHIND THE VEIL

*E*ach one of us has bits and pieces of his life's memories, the dreams of early childhood, and all the character-shaping factors. Yes, I remember every moment; I almost remember the moment I was born. This moment is stuck in my memory since my mother told me all about it. It was a Wednesday in 1971. I was the first-born baby girl to my parents. I was the first joy, the first baby crying in our home.

I am the eldest of four sisters. Our financial status was average like that of any ordinary family. I studied in public schools. My father did his best to provide for our needs. His dream was to give us a good education, especially me. We were all girls, so my dad wished to have a son. He spared no effort to let us have a good share of education and provide us with all our needs. As far as religion is concerned, we were raised with moral values and religious commitment.

My father is a true Muslim. Having been raised in the countryside, my father was keen to maintain all religious rituals and traditions. As for my mom, she was less conservative than my dad. She prayed every now and then. I can remember that mom had many arguments with dad concerning all the rituals and traditions. He wanted both of them to be a good example for us to follow in all religious matters. I remember that my dad used to get up early for the dawn prayer at a mosque in our hometown. Sometimes I would wake up to the voice of the 'azzan' (call to prayer). I was amazed by my father's persistence to pray the five obligatory prayers on time at the mosque. Nothing prevented him from doing that, not the cold of winter, the heat of summer, not even during his sickness.

I once asked him, "Why don't you pray at home in the cold weather?" His replied was by going out to the mosque in such bad weather, God would reward him with great compensation. Dad was, and still is, a conservative faithful Muslim.

When I was seven years old, my dad encouraged me to fast the whole month of Ramadan (Ramadan is one of the Islamic calendar months that all Muslim are obliged to fast). Then he proceeded to tell me one of the Hadiths (Prophet's tradition), "Teach them till the age of seven, and beat them till the age of ten."

I used to feel hungry during the long day of fasting, especially at that age, but I was faithful and patient till the end of the day. I managed to fast the whole month. My dad was very proud of my religious commitment and happily announced the news to all our family members.

I was very happy to achieve what I felt was a difficult task. My dad assured me that God would reward me according to His promise. Before the age of twelve I did not pray regularly and dad always argued with us about this matter. Discipline in both study and prayer were the two topics that pushed us into arguments and tongue-lashings in our life at home.

Dad had a way to punish us that I strongly rejected. If one of us didn't pray for any other reason than the legal reasons, he would refuse to eat with us at the same table according to the Prophet's tradition. I wondered how could the Prophet teach principles likely to cause family dissensions. What kind of a commitment was dad expecting to come out of such a punishment?

We grew up with the idea that Christians were infidels and polytheists not worthy of our friendship or companionship. There was one exception to that rule. One of my dad's friends was a Christian named Fawzy. They had a close relationship dad had known him since his childhood. I was always amazed when he, his wife and their son used to come to visit us on our joyful occasions and feasts. After they left, my dad would say: "Oh, Fawzy, it's a big waste for you to be a Christian. I wish you were a Muslim!"

At thirteen, I joined a prep school. On the first day of school all students usually ran and battled to get the best seats in class. A girl named Marcella sat beside me. This was a name that was not familiar to me. This was a new adventure for me to deal with an infidel Christian who sat at the same desk with me for the whole year. The funny thing is when I got to know her I found myself fascinated by her. I still remember there was an innocent beaming of her face. To this day, I still remember her tenderness as if it were yesterday and not many years ago.

I remember once she asked me what kind of sandwich I had for lunch. I replied that I had a Roman cheese sandwich. Marcella said she had a ham sandwich and asked if I would like to swap sandwiches. "Muslims do not eat pork, it is forbidden in Islam," was my immediate response to her suggestion. She asked me why. I told her, "God was protecting us from this meat that was not good for our health." She looked at me, her eyes wandering and resorted to silence. I honestly wondered if my answer was true and logical. I mean why didn't eating pork affect all these Christians year after year? I really didn't have an answer, nor did I bother searching for one, and soon I forgot the whole thing.

The first year of school passed and our friendship grew. The following year at school, one day Marcella was putting all her books on our table looking for something in her bag. One of those books was the Holy Bible. My curiosity was peaked like never before and I picked it up. My interest increased day by day. After that I asked her if I could have a look at this Holy Book. As I scanned the Book I saw the words; "Jesus of Nazareth went around doing good." I asked Marcella, "Who is this Jesus? Was He a person?" It was the fist time I heard His name.

Marcella said that He was the Christ. I closed the book and handed it to her. This phrase stuck in my mind and I had a burning desire to understand it. "A person going around doing good" – what a wonderful person – to be devoted to doing good! I went home with a deep longing to get a Bible to know more about that person. With the innocence of a child, I asked my father to get me a Bible and I told him what happened. And you can imagine what happened! A tremendous outburst of anger erupted in our home. My father made my face black and blue, while repeating two sentences over and over: "Christians are infidels...the Bible is corrupted." I cried, regretting what I did and repented. However, before long, the same desire came back. I finally asked Marcella to tell me about Jesus. She told me that how He loved everyone and did miracles to help people.

One day I attended our Islamic religion class. The teacher was a young man with the sign of prayer on his forehead. I had a desire to ask a question I had had in mind for a long time. I hesitated to ask because I knew it is forbidden to ask such a question, but I could no longer hold it. Finally, I got up my courage and said, "Teacher, can I ask a question? But I mean...may God forgive me." My tongue was released and I managed to utter the question: "Would it not be more reasonable if the Prophet Mohammed would have helped all the women in their difficult circumstances without marrying them? Would it not be more reasonable if he helped them without marriage being a condition? Would it not be more reasonable if he were not a polygamist?"

My answer was a slap on my face and the word "infidel!" It was the first time I got beaten at school. I felt that I was greatly insulted. I went to the school headmistress to complain and I told her what happened. I told her that I had all the right to ask. It was a common sense question. It was his duty as a religion teacher to answer me. I wondered why he accused me of being infidel? The headmistress was a fanatic. She always rebuked us for not wearing the veil, but she was also wise. She told me that if the Prophet had had relationships with them to help them, he would have caused them a lot of trouble and exposed them to rumors and suspicions. I nodded, but I was not really convinced. Her answer did not make amends for my insult. Realizing it was useless; I repented again and decided to just forget this subject.

My father used to push us to pray consistently, so I decided to commit myself to prayer. I realized that discussion and thinking were useless, so I decided to keep the five daily prayers as a duty in order to avoid my father's curses. I felt intimidated. In my first prostration I asked God to help me finish the last prostration and get done with this chore. I was not thinking of God, and my prayer did not bring any change in my character. My attitude towards Christians was still hostile, a result of the way we were brought up. Marcella was the only Christian I had exposure to. I even avoided passing by the Christian church near our home.

At home, things remained the same for a few years. Clashes and disputes went from bad to worse between my parents until they did what changed the course of their lives. It was 'the least recommended of the legitimate' as they said – to get separated.

I started to get a new role in my family. I was 16 when, in place of my dad, I had the responsibility as head of the family, caring for my four sisters. I had to focus on three things, namely to get high grades at school, to be a good mother to my sisters and to assume my father's responsibilities.

I did not allow myself to think of anything else. I finished my preparatory school with high grades. My dream was to pursue my university education, but for financial reasons and because I was caring for my family, my father did not allow me to go to high school. I started to feel that everything was against me. That feeling was one of rejection and rebellion. But there was no way out of this bad situation. Each year brought more grief, sorrow, and brokenness. I had nowhere to go!

This time I took refuge in God. After all, I had no other choice, but to seek God. I was so weak, so honest and in dire need of Him. I committed myself to pray and fast, and to follow all the Islamic ordinances. I started to wear the veil. After I finished each prayer, I used to call upon God and talk to Him a lot, but I felt that my prayers and supplications would hit the ceiling and come back to me with neither an answer nor help or even hope.

I always felt that God was far away from me, "as far as the East from the West." After I finished my education, I stayed more than two years at home. I was bored to death by such a routine life, so I started to look for a job. It came to my knowledge that a law office had a vacancy for a secretary.

The owner of this law office was a Christian. I was certain that my father would refuse such an idea, but I had to tell him. He categorically refused. When I persisted, finally my dad agreed. Working at a business owned by a Christian, my curiosity for the Christian religion started to increase.

I started by questioning him about a picture of the Virgin Mary on the wall behind him: "Where did you get it? Why did they say that Jesus was God while he was born of an ordinary woman, even if his birth was miraculous?" I hardly finished my question, when his anger flared and he said to me in a firm way, "At work there are no questions about religion! It is enough what is going on in the country nowadays!" He was referring to a terrible terrorist attacks that happened in 1991.

So fear and ignorance of his religion compelled that lawyer from getting involved in any discussion about religion. Ignorance and fear are more than enough to hide the most awesome beauty. So, I decided to learn more about Christianity from some Christian books in the library of our office. I started to read about the crucifixion, the trinity, and the Son of God and His love. I was fascinated by the great love story that appeared clearly with the cross and salvation. I found it to be logical to the mind and satisfactory to the soul. I had a fear about getting involved in such readings, so I stopped. I asked for help from an Islamic theologian in order to answer all my questions and to help me stop my attraction to Christ.

I went to the sheik of the mosque near my home and told him about my little satisfaction and my great fear. He gave me the solution to the sickness of searching for knowledge and gave me three steps I had to follow strictly:

First Step: stop reading about this religion and leave my work,

Second Step: repent, pray and fast three days; and

Third Step: keep on reading the Holy Qur'an everyday.

I did what the sheik requested except for leaving my work. I was afraid that my dad would not allow me to work again. When I started reading the Holy Qur'an, I found no healing of my disease. In fact, I began to discover something that increased my doubts and worries. A woman, according to the Qur'an, lacks the insight and the religious commitment, so the inheritance of a man is twice that of a woman!!

In court, the witness of two women is equal to that of one man (considering that women are less intelligent). So not one of us women could be a doctor, researcher, judge, philosopher, or even a wise person!!!

The majority of people condemned in hell will be women!! Moreover, lots of them will serve as hell's firewood. Just imagine – we women were created just to please men and eventually we will end up being the firewood of hell or nymphs of Jannah (beautiful women to please men in heaven.)

A woman in Islam should not leave her house except for one of three reasons: to move to her husband's house, to perform the Hajj, or to be buried. I was tired of all the Qur'anic verses that talked about fights in Islam and the seas of blood that were still being shed in the name of religion. Try to imagine that after twenty-one years of strongly believing in something, it turns out to be false. It was the most difficult time I have ever had. How could someone who used to take refuge in God all of a sudden live without a refuge and without a god?

After a month of sleepless nights, of weeping and crying, and of waiting upon the true God to descend from heaven to earth to answer me, I got tired of thinking. I then went back to reading the Qur'an, which left me more bewildered and confused. So, I decided to read the Holy Bible that I might find the truth.

But people said that the original version of the Holy Bible did not exist any more. What could I do? I had no choice but to read this corrupted version of the Bible that I may find the truth between the lines. So I started to read the Holy Bible and I discovered Jesus, the name that I had heard about long ago, and the name I had been attracted to. I saw how he healed the sick, freed the captives, forgave the adulterous woman, loved and blessed his enemies. For the first time in my life I discovered what I had never experienced – the fatherhood heart or the motherhood care – because my parents were separated long ago and I was the eldest daughter.

Now I feel that Jesus is my father and mother. I have felt Him hugging me, holding me in His arms like a baby. He took away all the heavy loads that burdened me. For the first time in my life, I felt that I was a real woman – a real person, really beloved; not a commodity to please men, but created after the image of God. I cried like someone who had been rescued from hell or death. On that day I said to Jesus, "Jesus, you are my God and my Savior. You are my father and my mother; you are everything to me in life."

From that day, I turned over a new leaf, full of events, miracles, and persecution, but we will talk about that later.

Yours,

Leila

BLESS THE
PEOPLE OF EGYPT

*M*y name is Mozafar. I was born in 1969. I was the first born to a middle class family that lived in a beautiful quiet city. I grew up to be responsible. I was different from the other children. I did not play that much or hang around on the streets like other kids.

My dad worked in another town, so I had to take care of my two brothers – Hassan, the middle one and Anwar, the youngest. I had to play the role of my absent father most of the time. Financially, we were well to do. I even went to private school. Many years passed with no trouble for me or my family. We were Muslims that prayed, fasted and observed the religious ordinances in a moderate way, free from fanaticism or fundamentalism.

One day, questions arose in my mind that totally changed my life from an ordinary one to a life full of surprises and changes. It was the day I started high school. That period is very important to everyone, for in that time of one's, life there is a search for one's identity and to question things taken for granted.

Each of us had inherited his/her religion, color, language, race and gender. No one had chosen any of these factors, important as they are. We are dealing with this unavoidable inheritance, with God and with others. For example, we as Muslims are born and raised to hate Jews and Christians, and to believe that Muslims are the best nation in the world. No one could ever imagine that the others (Jews, Christians, etc.) could be right at all. The idea of others being right never even crossed our mind.

Very few people would ever consider examining the things we inherited, let alone questioning how right this inheritance was. If we ask others (Jews and Christians) to examine their inheritance and correct it, it means that we are very sure that they are wrong, and we consider them blind because they accept their inheritance without examination. It would be appropriate if we would do what we asked of others. (It's logical that you treat people the same way you would have them treat you.) I think that examining our inheritance and trying to discover the truth would make us deeply rooted in the good areas and more flexible to change the areas of ignorance and vanity. For sure, the true God loves the people who search for the truth, the light, the good, and the better life.

The time of high school started with new friendships in this new school which was full of surprises and diversity. I think that my generation will be remembered throughout the school's history. I got to know atheist students who did not believe in the existence of God, students from the violent Islamic fundamental groups, and other students who enjoyed their adolescent lives and cared for nothing but girls. It was a very different and complex variety for me. It was a big leap from a normal, almost boring life to a very rich life in quantity and quality.

I started to develop some friendships and I got to know a person who became a close friend of mine in a very short time. After almost 16 years of our friendship, I realize that anyone who has not experienced such a friendship remains lonely, knowing nothing about a warm relationship, companionship, honesty, and faithfulness. Such a person would never get to know others because he has never gotten to know himself. Forgive me; I am very fanatical about friendships.

My new friend, Basil, had similar thoughts about humanity and its sole source traced back our father, Adam and our mother, Eve. He also believed that brotherhood and friendship were the feelings that should govern all human relationships. It is the only feeling that surpasses all the illusion and the real barriers of beliefs, language, color, gender and social class. He used to say that if all human beings would consider that all of us had the same origin, the world would have become happier, avoiding wars, famines and struggles. The world would have become a little house belonging to a big family, where peace, justice, equality, and freedom prevailed.

These principles were our main concern even in our emotional relationship. We believed in Platonic love, the love that reveres the spirit and pays no attention to the desires of the flesh. Those moments, days and years were really beautiful. We were idealistic adolescents who had the hearts of children, innocence and curiosity. Utopia was our dream day and night.

I remember we spent many nights in discussion and reading. My family had another apartment besides the one we lived in. That apartment was a hideout for Basil and me. We used to spend a lot of time writing, listening to our favorite songs, and reading all kinds of books, permitted or banned. We were attracted to banned books such as, *God, Don't Let Me into Heaven if it has Walls!* by Salah Jahin, not cigarettes or drugs.

My friend, Basil raised many questions. I remember he used to say that Islam's claim that Judaism and Christianity were corrupted was likely to destroy all religions, including Islam itself. I used to ask him: "How? Islam is the only religion that is protected, and preserved." I used to quote the famous Qur'anic verse:

"We have, without doubt, sent down the Message; and we will assuredly guard it (from corruption)." (Surah 15:9)

He used to say, "We believe these words because we are Muslims. Not one of us tries to look to the case of corruption in a neutral, objective way, that is, "Did God send down the Torah (the Old Testament) and Zabour (the Psalms) and the Bible (the New Testament)?" When I responded with, "Yes," Basil then asked, "Is there anyone who could change or modify God's words?"

I quoted to him the verses proclaiming that there was no modification or alteration in God's words. No human being or even an angle could do so, because God is the Omnipotent, the Almighty, and the most Powerful and He can protect His Books.

Then Basil would say, "You believe that God is the Omnipotent, the Almighty, and the most Powerful, and no one could change His words; so how could He allow this corruption to happen not only in one of His Books, but in all His Books except for one? How could He allow the Old Testament sent down to Moses to be corrupted? How could He allow the Zabour (Psalms) sent down to David to be altered? And, after all, how could God allow the Bible (the New Testament) sent down to Isa to be altered?

Is it possible after almost 600 years, six whole centuries – generations having lived and died in deception and distortion of the Holy Books – that God would bring a Book that nobody can corrupt?

All of a sudden God has become Omnipotent, Almighty, keeping His words from corruption! After a long history in which His Books were corrupted and His servants had gone astray, i.e. the children of Israel who were God's most favored nation, and the priests and monks who would recite the Book, enjoy what is right, and forbid what is bad! Is it possible that all of them have gone astray? Can you imagine that God, who could not protect His Book from being distorted, altered, and corrupted, could protect His worshipers?

I used to think silently, and I had no answer. I knew that the point was not to find a solution or an answer to save God from that puzzle that He had caused.

I knew that Basil's questions were genuine and logical. I knew that he was sincere in seeking God and not worldly pleasures. He would ask me why Muslims claimed that the Holy Books were corrupted but, at the same time, insisted that the Qur'an was preserved – as if the Qur'an were God's only Book. Does God favor some Books over others, or prophets over others?

Didn't God care about the generations of mankind who died in their false beliefs, thinking that they were true? How could God let them dedicate their lives to following these Books wholeheartedly if they were really corrupted? I don't believe that the true God would discriminate between His Books or His prophets. He would not discriminate between Arabs and non-Arabs except regarding their heart's intentions. Therefore, we have to ask these questions not only to Jews and Christians, but also to God Almighty Himself.

I felt that Basil was always sincere. I recall the nights we spent reading the three Books – the Torah, the Bible and the Qur'an – trying to find similarities and differences among them. We had a great time, even though it was mentally and emotionally exhausting. It is not easy to be neutral and objective in research. There is nothing easier than to proclaim a certain religion right or wrong without a real search, a search that would satisfy the seeker and God as well.

Basil used to ask me, "Which comes first, the authentic currency or the counterfeit one?" I would answer that it was the authentic that came first followed by the counterfeit. He responded, "That's logical, but how could God allow His first three Books to be corrupted and only keep His fourth Book (the Qur'an) intact? What is the standard that we use to check out corruption: the earlier Books or the later Books?" Basil challenged me, "Forgive me, my friend, but how would someone who allowed His Books to be corrupted ask us to trust His fourth Book?"

Could you believe that I accepted these bold questions from Basil without feeling that he mocked God or the Qur'an? I knew that he really loved God and respected people. He was just thinking fairly, honestly and objectively. He used to say; "In the afterlife, nothing will help us, but the truth." Basil would raise common sense questions such as: "How were the Holy Books corrupted? When? Where? And who did it?"

These were the kind of questions no Muslim, in the past or present time, cared to exert any effort to answer. The issue of corruption is as clear as broad daylight. Only an ignorant person would overlook it.

My friend, Basil was more interested than me in the matters of religion and the afterlife. One evening as we sat talking and discussing things, suddenly Basil and I had an idea at the same time (like that 'telepathy' we heard about.) The idea was to write a booklet containing our principles, dreams, thoughts, dialogues and beautiful memories.

It was a special dream that started that evening in 1986 – an evening to remember! The booklet's title was to be 'We Don't Believe.' Its main idea was to explain what we didn't believe in and why. I remember one sentence from the introduction of the booklet: "We are captives of our customs, traditions, common feelings and incapable senses…"

One day Basil came to meet me. I saw in his eyes something I had never seen before. He looked like someone who carried a secret that he could no longer bear. I felt that his eyes were revealing that secret, even before his tongue could do so. He started pacing back and forth, talking like someone who was thinking aloud and not talking to me in particular. It was a unique speech!

"You know that for a long time I have been searching and reading all the Holy Books and secular books. I have always tried to remain objective. I seek nothing but God. I have no intention to lift up a certain religion above the others for any reason.

After a long time of studious search and sleepless nights, looking for a moment of safety and a father's heart to welcome back the prodigal son, I have to tell you that the road of searching is not rosy. On the contrary, many times I felt myself drowning in a flood of questions with no answers. Sometimes I was about to abandon my objectivity and just embrace any religion, like a drowning man holding to any straw, but I could not deny that the power of the Almighty surrounded me. When I hit rock bottom, totally frustrated, I could feel a new hope infiltrating my soul, giving me new strength to lift me up and guide my steps on the way.

Every morning I renewed my commitment to seek the goal and to persevere until I discovered the truth. I had to find the God who would reconcile me with heaven, with myself, and with other people – all other people, friends and enemies alike. I was looking for a God who could change my heart, even create a new heart in me – a heart that knows how to praise Him, to have mercy, to forgive, to care, to shine and to change the world for the better!

Would you believe it, my friend? I've found that wonderful, great God! He is my Savior, my God, my crown, my strength, my Lord, my cause and my struggle – Jesus Christ!"

I knew Basil very well and was familiar with his progressive thoughts, but nevertheless I was shocked to hear that he had abandoned Islam to become an apostate. My close friend, whom I love, had abandoned Islam and become an infidel. I could not talk to him. He realized my shock and left me alone to reconsider our friendship and my own personal search.

I was worried and felt that doubt was infiltrating my inherited beliefs. I felt my roots were being pulled out. I thought in my heart that I had been trapped by doubts because I did not study and follow my religion the way I should have. I thought if I studied Islam and fulfilled all its commandments and optional rules I would have answers for all my questions. Only then would doubts disappear from my heart and be replaced by a deep belief in Islam, my religion as well as my father's. Afterwards, I would be able to guide my friend, Basil who had gone astray and become an infidel.

As a matter of fact, I went to Basil and told him what I thought. I was surprised to hear his answer. He did not reject what I said or me. He was not even upset. On the contrary, he was happy to hear about my decision as if he wanted me to study and follow Islam, and to become a true Muslim in the full sense of the word.

Basil actually encouraged me when he said to me, "The truth does not belong to man, but man belongs to the truth. God would never let someone who honestly seeks him go astray. Therefore, I am not concerned about you, or about myself. Continue with your plans and follow Islam, and may God grant you success. But be careful, Mozafar; good intentions are not enough to reach the shore of truth. Good intentions together with impartial and fair search, combined with diligent determination will carry you through safely. God will show you the way, the truth and the better life…"

So, I started a life of strict commitment and in-depth studies of Islam. I joined an Islamic group called "The Ancestors Group." We observed all the obligatory prayers at the mosque, attended the doctrine studies and went out calling on the young people to the life of Islamic commitment. Occasionally, the brothers and I would go on a retreat for a few days, sometimes a week, to worship and pray at other mosques in different cities.

We used to set up camps to recite the Qur'an. We discussed contemporary religious and political issues relevant to our group. These activities were under the supervision of university professors and highly educated professionals (physicians, engineers, lawyers, teachers, etc.)

I used to order my mother and my female relatives to wear the complete veil (the Islamic dress for women). I used to command all my friends to observe prayers at the exact time. All my relationships changed, except my friendship with Basil. Religiously speaking we were poles apart. He was an infidel apostate, but humanly speaking, he was my only friend that I couldn't abandon.

He was an infidel because he became a Christian, but he was honest, sincere, faithful and loving towards everyone. I used to pray to God to guide Basil back to Islam. I remember the brothers at "The Ancestors Group" always asked me to end my relationship with him because he was an infidel. Basil faced a lot of persecution because it was known in our city that he had become a Christian.

Nevertheless, I always saw Basil as both firm and friendly. He even showed love and forgiveness towards his persecutors. I was amazed and surprised at the same time. I had so many questions tearing up my mind: "How could he be full of such peace and love, being an infidel? How come he did not pay them back evil for evil – an eye for an eye and a tooth for a tooth?"

I remembered that he used to say that he followed in the steps of the Christ and believed in loving his enemies and forgiving those who mistreated him. Before such love, all my years of Islamic commitment and fundamentalism hardened me against his heart and his love diminished.

This love confronted all my claims and me. The claim that mine was the true religion, that Allah was the God of the universe. That Muslims were the best nation in the whole world and that our Prophet, Mohammed, was the seal of all Prophets and Messengers of God. All these claims could not stand in the face of that overflowing river of love. It made me run back to my ritual commitment, hoping that one day I would change and become stronger than Basil and his God. I could then face them and defeat them.

After two whole years of Islamic strict commitment and sincere search, I discover something that shook my whole being and made me doubt like never before. I found out that all Islamic worship commandments were not the result of the Islamic divine inspiration. They all existed in Arabia before Mohammed and the Qur'an. I also found out that the 'Sharia' (Islamic law) and all punishments were practiced before Islam. Many Islamic teachings were taken from the Torah, such as stoning an adulteress and cutting off the hand of a thief, etc.

I also found out that true Christianity was completely different from what Islam pictured it to be. Islam attacked Christianity, claiming that Christians believed in three gods. I was taught that God married Mary and gave birth to Jesus, the son of gods. Islam also claimed that Christians worshipped Jesus and Mary as gods, apart from the true God. I discovered that all these things were false. They were taken from the superstitions prevailing in Arabia before and during the age of Mohammed.

True Christianity believed in one God six centuries before Islam, and brought along sublime principles and teachings, which no human being can face but with reverence. After four years of studies, discussion, search and commitment in "The Ancestors Group," combined with sleepless nights and tearful eyes asking God to lead me to the right way, I decided to stop and reconsider everything in my life. On the other hand, I had another problem. I was committed to join my group every day at the mosque for prayers and studies. How could I suddenly drop out? How could I shave my beard and abandon the Islamic dress code (Galabia)? And so many other questions…

What would they think, considering that I had a relationship with Basil, who had become a Christian? They would say that I, too, became a Christian like him. That would cause me a lot of trouble and persecution. I had no choice but to overcome my fears and face the truth with logic and wisdom this time. After four years of studious search, I had no choice but to accept the results whatever it may cost.

So, I stopped all my activities and asked God to show me the right way. At that time, I was more doubtful of Islam and more convinced of Christ. For four years, my friend, Basil spared no effort to explain all the issues and problems that I faced concerning Christianity. Every day he would, tirelessly and confidently, speak with me about Christ. I was almost ready to accept Christ as God and Savior, but there was something inside me that did not yet embrace this faith. I still was not filled with that faith in Christ. I told Basil that I did not know the reason behind it.

He said, "I would not know either, but do you believe that God knows everything, and He is the only one that can answer you and satisfy all you hunger for the truth?" I said 'Yes.' He then said, "I do, too. Let's pray and ask God to reveal Himself to you in a clear way. The God we believe in is real and close. He hears our prayers and talks with us. He is not an illusion He is alive and can interact with us."

I agreed with Basil and started to pray, asking God to clearly reveal Himself to me, to guide me and to quench my thirst to the truth. One cold night in March 1988, I spent all night praying with tears till dawn. I poured out my heart and all the four years of pain and struggle. I still remember that night twenty years ago as if it was yesterday. It was a night in the Holy of Holies after four years of exhaustion and insecurity. I had always tried to please God in order to feel that He was with me and close to me even for just one moment. However, the more I committed to Islam the lonelier I felt. The more I obeyed, the more worried I became; the more pious I got, the more scared I felt. Four years without peace, safety or security. My claim that the God of Islam was closer to us than ourselves seemed unfounded.

Even though I had not yet confessed Christ as my God, I just came close to him and touched the hem of his teachings. He lifted my heart up towards him and compensated me for the years of poverty, loneliness and bitterness. He filled me with joy, peace and a certain serenity that I could not explain...something I had never experienced before in my life.

In that early morning I wanted to run to all my family members, my friends and my acquaintances and to tell them about the treasure that I discovered – the real God I had found in Jesus Christ who loved me before I loved Him.

I ran to Basil and told him my whole story as if he did not know it. He listened while his tears were streaming down his face. He praised God for me like a mother receiving her son or a father waiting four years for the return of his prodigal son.

Yours,

Mozafar

FROM THE HOMELAND OF CHRIST

THE CHILDREN OF ISHMAEL WILL RETURN

I was born in the homeland of Christ, the beloved Palestine. We are the so-called "Arabs of the West Bank." I was born in the late fifties under the dark shadow of the Occupation. I lived in a country that was not my homeland, but who can choose his or her time of birth or death?

My family consists of seven boys and four girls. My father passed away when I was eight years old. My heart was filled with sadness: birth with no homeland and a child with no father. I felt as if heaven was hostile towards me. I think that childhood is the time that forms our image of God for each of us. I think by now you can imagine the characteristics of my God.

My village is located near "Al-Quds" (Jerusalem) – Jerusalem that killed the prophets and stoned those sent to her, Jerusalem that crucified the Christ.

When you are born in "Al-Quds" (Jerusalem), you become a commando who has been tamed, and a child not unlike the revolutionary children throwing stones at the enemy occupying the land. But who can imprison the spirit and the heart? Even prisons cannot do that, or the Occupation.

Therefore, I carried the heart, spirit, and revolution of the 'Children of Stones' even though I have not seen a single demonstration or any kind of "Intifada" (uprising) in my village.

But I remember when I was a child; I would soar high in my daydreams, daydreams in which I was to liberate Palestine. These dreams of liberation always ended up with me being martyred.

I was really a Palestinian child in the full meaning of the term, even with the Occupation's attempts to brainwash the Arab youth to forget their roots, their homeland, as well as the cry of their mothers.

In fact, sadness became a language we learned from our early childhood. Helpless and trapped in every way: from earning a living, to finding shelter, at school, and in the street. We are not like the children of the Jews. Discrimination is obvious in everything. If the Occupation forces discriminate between Eastern Jews and Western Jews, how would they not discriminate against us?

All these things were shaping me as well as my faith in God. God was my first and last refuge. I prayed and fasted until I was 15 years old, but what was the result?

What happened? Did a miracle happen to set us free?

Did our homeland return to us?

Did God raise our martyrs from the graves?

Did God return our lost happiness or put an end to our shed blood?

Did God return the exiles to their homeland?

Millions of question exploded inside me against our fate that heaven has destined us to face. Why did death, genocide, banishment, and imprisonment become our destiny set apart from other nations and peoples? Is it the will of heaven? The answer in my heart of hearts was in the affirmative.

Therefore, I rejected this fate, this destiny and this God. I lived for four years not believing in any god. Flagrant atheism lives in the heart and is proclaimed by words and deeds. So, my life lost its meaning. All morals and principles withered in me. In fact, I committed all the sins and transgressions, the big ones as well as the small ones.

Then something happened! It was the beginning of change in my life. I happened to meet a European young lady. Her name was Tina. She was in Al-Quds (Jerusalem) for a year. We got to know each other and became good friends. She was not one of the ordinary people that you meet every day. On the contrary, she was a unique person of a rare type – the type that, if you got to know them, you would never forget. She was a human being in the full sense of the word, beaming with life and special presence – a presence that makes you feel important, and that you are a civilized person, and that time is precious. Yes, she is truly a woman with whom you feel all of a sudden that everything has meaning and value.

Tina spoke four languages fluently. She always said that there was no comparison between the Spring and Summer of Europe and those of Al-Quds with its beautiful gardens and flowery fields. Tina started to feel concerned because she was getting attracted to a Muslim man. She knew that hers was a very conservative, traditional Christian family and they would never approve of such a relationship.

Tina started planning to go back home. She had already spent a year in Al-Quds – a year that flew by like a day! I also started planning to travel to Europe, which made Tina very happy. In July 1979, I actually visited her in Europe. She was my tour guide. I remember visiting her family, who welcomed me warmly.

We spoke once about the habit of eating pork in Europe and the Western countries. Tina said something that astonished me. She told me that the Lord Jesus Christ said that what made a man unclean was not food or drink, but what came out of the heart and his intentions!

During this visit we dotted the I's and crossed the T's in our relationship. We realized that we were not just friends, but also romantic lovers. So, we decided to get married. As for me, getting married wasn't an easy decision, but rather it was the first milestone of the long journey of taking responsibility.

When I went back to Al-Quds to prepare for our marriage, my mother was anxiously waiting for me. My mother is a conservative Muslim with a strong personality. My mother told me that she opposed my travel to Europe to get married, and that Tina should come to Al-Quds, so it would be an Islamic marriage according to the law of God and His Prophet. It was common in Palestine that if a Western woman married a Muslim man she automatically became a Muslim, wore the veil, and learned the Arabic language and the Qur'an.

At that same time Tina repented and renewed her relationship with her God and Savior Jesus Christ. She became a Christian in the full meaning of the term and became a true believer. After preparing everything, I traveled to Europe and we got married. Our marriage was actually the most important and wonderful step I have ever taken in my life.

Tina did not fall into the category of typical Christian wives who are married to non-believer husbands; that is, she did not preach at me day and night or rebuke me for my evil and negative deeds from her point of view. She did not even make me feel inferior to her. She was a godly wife and an encouragement toward changing and reflecting God's own image.

She was submissive to me. She knew how to treat an Eastern man who is very proud, protective of his self-esteem, opinion and manhood. All these virtues of hers affected me, but didn't totally change me. I was still leading a sinful life. I would get drunk and spend all night in bars, which made me very moody.

What suffering Tina had with me! It was beyond the capacity of any human being, but she was really a woman like Jesus. I wish I only got drunk, but I even used all kinds of drugs. My years were spent in slavery to the Devil, but in the middle of thorns stood a firm flower with a never-ending love – my wife, Tina. I was proud of her faith and morals before all people. I was lost for five years, as if anticipating death, as if I was slowly putting myself to death. Tina was praying for me. She was asking God to save and rescue me.

She could not be silent and she could not let God keep silent either. In fact, Heaven answered her prayer on the last day of 1984. I was staggering on the street after a long night of drinking when a person met me and invited me to his house to have a cup of tea. I was drunk, but I agreed to go with him that night.

We talked for a couple of hours or more. The next morning I remembered nothing, but a little part of our conversation. I remembered that he had asked me about my belief in God and that I answered him saying, "Yes, I believe in God, His Messengers and Prophets: Moses, Isa and Mohammed." He said, "I know only one way to heaven. It is through our God and Savior Jesus Christ, who has completed reconciliation between God and man. Without Jesus Christ you cannot enter heaven no matter how good you are or how much you give to charity." Then he asked me to read the Gospel of John. I also remembered that I was mad at him when I left, but I liked his boldness and honesty. I invited him to my home and I gave him my address. We set an appointment for the following Friday.

I actually looked for my wife's Bible. I started to read the Gospel of John. I read it several times. I tried to be well prepared for our Friday conversation. On the following Friday, I decided to stop drinking to be fully awake during the conversation.

He came accompanied with another person named Nels. They started to talk to me about God's love for me and for all nations, how God cared for each one of us, and how the selfishness and evils of man brought about all the suffering on earth – the fallen earth.

God is not pleased with the evil of man or the results of that evil. God does not want us to go through the sufferings that we cause ourselves. A man reaps what he sows. God, the true love, does not tempt anyone with evil. God is the source of good, virtue, holiness, and providence. I listened attentively. My heart was thirsty.

With my wife and the Bible, I met with these two men quite often, to the extent that religion had become my preoccupation after long years of wasting my life.

Tina wanted me to come to know Christ, the Awaited Messiah of the Old Testament (Al Torah). She wanted to prove to me that Christ is the center of the Old Testament and the New Testament, the center of the Divine Inspiration. Tina knew that I was fluent in Hebrew, the language of the Old Testament. She started to quote all the prophecies that spoke about the Christ. Almost three hundred prophecies spoke about the Christ, His miraculous birth, His life, His suffering, His crucifixion, His death, and His wonderful resurrection. I discovered that all these existed hundreds and thousands of years before Christ.

This discovery shook my whole being. I was puzzled to see the Jews not believing in the Christ (the Awaited Messiah) though they read the Old Testament every day. It is actually God who guides and not the mindless recitations.

I began to realize that Christ is not an ordinary person. He is the core of the Old Testament and the Jews are still waiting for Him. We Muslims are also waiting for the Christ as a just ruler to judge all nations. Christians are certainly waiting for the Christ as a 'god' and a king. Who is this person anticipated by all nations, by Jews, Christians, and Muslims?

If Jesus were an ordinary man, He would have taken more than He deserved when compared with other religions that have other prophets like Moses in the Old Testament and Mohammed in Islam. It would have been more appropriate for the Jews to wait for Moses and the Muslims for Mohammed, but this was not the case and everybody is still waiting for Jesus Christ.

Even the miracles that Christ performed were different from those of other Prophets. Not that the difference was one of prophetic messages or recipients, but rather that Christ was the only Prophet who resembled God in His divine attributes and power to the extent of being one and the same. So, how can God give a prophet – whatever his status or message may be – such a privilege, that is, the privilege of being a partner with God, not only in His attributes, power and holiness, but also in His love?

My inner struggle came to a head even though I was not a fanatic Muslim. I was an infidel most of the time. How powerful religion in the East is! It is deeply rooted in our genes, blood cells, and bone marrow. There is nothing more difficult than changing one's beliefs that have been engraved throughout the years of childhood and upbringing.

I was thinking – if the good deeds really outweigh the bad deeds, I would need another life to do enough good deeds to erase my evil ones. Therefore, there is no way for me to be saved by good deeds or charities. Who will rescue me from my sins and vanities? Who will save me then?

At that time, I was unaware that the love of Christ was growing in me, and finally I could not bear the struggle any more, so I cried out to God, "Let me know the truth. Where is the real and true religion? Heavenly religions believe that you are one, but the question is, are you still far away from us in the seventh heaven or have you incarnated and drawn near us and in unity with us?"

I also said to him, "Oh, Jesus Christ, if you are really my God and Savior, change my life and turn my black heart into a white one, from a heart full of hatred to a heart full of love, from an unclean heart to a heart full of holiness, purity, and cleanness." My life actually started to change in a way I never dreamed of. I started to experience a joy that filled my inner being – without drugs or any kind of alcohol. My whole life started to change.

Now I have clear goals, principles, and a new meaning of life. Now there's a God I am ready to lose everything for. He is all sufficient for me. Finally my wife rejoiced, for she saw the harvest of her tears and prayers. Now our home has become a church, the bride of Christ. We started a new life, a life of service, miracles, and great testimony. We will talk about it some other time for the glory of Jesus Christ!

Yours,

Khalil

Repentance in Front of a Mosque

*T*his is the account of my conversion to Christianity. My name is Abraham. I am so proud of my Arabic name because it is the name of the great Patriarch. My new name is Timothy, but that does not change the fact that I am Abraham, nicknamed 'Abu-Khalil,' the son of a couple of simple peasants. I was raised in a humble place, where we had reeds for a carpet, an oil lamp for light and hard cheese for food. I used to study my lessons by the little stream wearing my white 'Galabia.' I still wear 'Galabia' up till now.

When I was a little child, my mom took me by the hand and brought me to the village 'Kottab' (Islamic learning place), where a Sheikh taught us reading, writing and reciting the Qur'an. He charged us a whole dime at the end of each week. At the 'Kottab' my mind and heart were filled with obedience for God, the Creator of heaven and earth.

When I joined the prep school (junior high) I became more interested in 'Dhekr' sessions (mystical worship) at the mosque. I started attending the mystical sessions of the village's Sufi group. We used to praise the Prophet Mohammed to the point of not being aware of our surroundings, repeating "Oh, Messenger of God, help!"

One day after the sunset prayers at the Station's mosque, two men came up to me and introduced themselves. One was named 'Mohammed,' the other 'Solomon.' They greeted me in a pious, friendly way and I saw in them a unique kindness and real desire to please God. They introduced me to the rest of their friends. They loved one another and encouraged each other to obey God. I was impressed by their unity. They were the elite of our town's young men. They had noticed my dedication to worshipping God and my public speaking skills.

The first Monday of each of the Arabic months, our group had a meeting where I used to deliver a speech after the sermon of the 'Emir' (prince of the group). I actually started preaching in mosques when I was only 14 years old. I guess it was okay since, Imam Shafai, used to give 'Fatwa' (religious advice) when he was 6 or 9 years old. I remember my first sermon at the mosque was about the ideal way to celebrate the Prophet's birthday. We used to fast and eat together at the mosque, following the steps of the Prophet Mohammed, even in the minutest details, such as in the manner of walking, talking, praying, eating, drinking, dressing, etc.

I am indebted to these people because they encouraged me to read, search and research. These factors actually brought me to where I am today. One day, a friend of mine said to my father, "Abraham is one of the public speakers of the Sunni Group; he attends all their public and secret meetings." I was surprised and upset because that man was the same person who encouraged me to commit to the Islamic call and to join the Muslim brethren group. We used to go together from one mosque to another, proclaiming the Islamic call. I always wished that my father had been present when I delivered my sermon.

After my secret was revealed, my dad started to warn me and threaten me many times, hoping that I would change my mind and leave the Muslim brethren group. Our group became well known to an informant named Mohammed. He used to follow all our news and movements and report them to the State Security Investigations office (SSI). He used to tape all our speeches and deliver them to the local SSI office. I was proud to see Mohammed taping my speeches at the mosque.

On the other hand, my father and I were not pleased that the SSI had gotten my name. My father was so concerned about my safety that he went to the Muslim brethren group at the mosque and screamed at them in front of everyone and asked them to leave me alone. He then came back and hit me and broke my teeth. One of my front teeth is still broken, a reminder of my days with the Muslim brethren.

For the first time in my life, my father burned all my religious books. He was so concerned about me and afraid that I might get hurt because of the Sunni Group. He even threatened to divorce my mother if I continued to go to the Sunni mosque. I asked him to allow me to just sit outside the mosque so that I could listen to the Muslim brethren sheikhs without actually going into the mosque. He agreed on the condition that he should go with me. We used to sit outside the mosque and I listened attentively.

Threats did not deter me from spreading the Islamic call. At school, I used to deliver an Islamic public speech every morning. I forced my sister to wear the veil. I stopped shaking hands with women and listening to songs for fear of God's punishment on Doomsday – punishment in the form of hot lead to be poured into the ears. My neighbors made fun of me for being so meticulous in applying all the commands of the Qur'an and Sunnah to the letter. It was not my fault; I had been taught that Islam was relevant and valid for every age and every country, and that Islam was the solution!

While striving to spread the Islamic call, I had an idea. I thought I should win my Christian friends to Islam so that we all would go to the Jannah (heaven). At that time, if you had asked me my opinion of Christians, I would have told you that they were infidels and polytheists, but I found out that the Qur'an itself taught otherwise.

In Surah 5: 82 the Qur'an says:

"Strongest among men in enmity to the believers wilt thou find the Jews and Pagans; and nearest among them in love to believers wilt thou find those who say, "We are Christians" because amongst these are men devoted to

REPENTANCE IN FRONT OF A MOSQUE

learning, and men who have renounced the world, and they are not arrogant."

According to this verse, the Qur'an made a distinction between Christians and infidels; if Christians were to be seen as infidels, the Qur'an would have put them in the same category.

In Surah 2: 62 the Qur'an says:

"And the Christians and the Sabians – any who believe in Allah and the Last Day, and work righteousness, shall have their reward with their Lord; on them shall be no fear, nor shall they grieve."

I tried to convince the Christians I met at school or in my neighborhood that Islam was the true religion. I even corresponded with some Christians in order to convert them to Islam. As a result, I had a burning desire in my heart to compare Islam and Christianity, to find out, once and for all, which was right and which was wrong; which was God's way and which was the Devil's way.

For two years I had been struggling. Many times I decided to end this internal battle by stopping the reading of Christian books, by focusing on reciting the Qur'an every morning, and by following the example of the Prophet Mohammed. I wanted to find peace and to obey God through the true religion. Therefore, I got rid of all my Christian books in order to become a real Muslim dedicated to the one true God, Allah.

But God did not leave me alone. His Holy Spirit used to stir me up in my sleep. Whenever I went to bed I got edgy. My conscience was restless. I could not sleep for nights on end. I wondered, "If Mohammed were really the Seal of Prophets, why would he not come at the end days instead of Christ as the just judge? In this case, Mohammed would be one of the signs of the Last Day and not Christ." I wondered about the secret behind Christ's supreme status among all prophets so much so that he became the center of history. "Do we not say that a certain historic event took place before Christ (B.C.) and another after Christ (A.D.)? What is the secret of your glory, Isa, son of Mary?"

These questions, and many more, made me strike a comparison between Christ and Mohammed. After spending a long time comparing them, I found out it was an unfair comparison, even in the Qur'an itself. In the Qur'an we never find Christ asking God's forgiveness for any sin or guilt, as did the rest of the prophets and messengers. Christ was right when he challenged the Jewish leaders saying, *"Can any of you prove me guilty of sin?"* (John. 8:46). He even rebuked the Jews for their false piety when they caught the adulterous woman in the act: *"If any one of you is without sin, let him be the first to throw a stone at her."* (John 8:7)

On the other hand, I found from the Qur'an itself that Mohammed was just a human being like any other, with his sins, his hostility towards the infidels and his death. The Qur'an says:

"And ask forgiveness for thy fault, and for the men and women who believe." (Surah 47:19)

"That Allah may forgive thee thy faults of the past and those to follow…" (Surah 48:2)

"And had We not given thee strength, thou wouldst nearly have inclined to them a little." (Surah 17: 74)

In his Qur'an commentary, Imam El-Syouty explained the reasons behind Surah 17:74:

"According to Mohammed, son of Kaab, from the tribe of Karz, the Prophet Mohammed recited Surah 53 until he said, "Have you seen 'Lat' and 'Uzza'…" (Names of idols), then the Devil made him say that Muslims could worship them, and that the idols' intercessions were to be sought. So, it became a verse in the Qur'an.

Prophet Mohammed was so sad about what happened until God inspired him with another verse:

"Never did we send a messenger or a prophet before thee, but, when he framed a desire, Satan threw some (vanity) into his desire; but Allah will cancel anything (vain) that Satan threw in, and Allah will confirm (and establish) His signs" (Surah 22:52).

That was the reason for Surah 17:73-74:

"And their purpose was to tempt thee away from that which We had revealed unto thee, to substitute in Our

Name something quite different: Behold! They would certainly have made thee (their) friend. And had We not given thee strength, thou wouldst nearly have inclined to them a little."

I could not find any verse in the Bible that said that Christ almost joined the infidels if it hadn't been for God's providence. The reason behind this fact, as I learned from my studies, was that Christ was the Word of God. The New Testament, which was written originally in the Greek language, states that Christ is the Word of God in the sense of 'the spoken mind of God.' Christ is the mind of God. God and God's mind are the same entity and the same essence, without any difference, division or separation. Christ is the Incarnated Word, God who came in the flesh. His divine nature has never departed from His human nature, not even for a moment or a twinkle of an eye.

All these thoughts bounced in my mind and fought in my heart. I was afraid of God's wrath that came upon infidels. Whenever I knelt down for prayers, I screamed from the bottom of my heart, "Oh, God, show me the truth. If Mohammed is right, I will follow him until I die; if Christ is right, I will follow him until I die. I would give my whole life to you and serve you all my life, whatever the cost maybe…"

I kept repeating this prayer until Christ came to me in a vision, in a dream. He said to me in His kind voice, "I love you." I meditated on the unending love of Christ and His sacrificial death on the cross to save and redeem us. With tears running down my face I said to Christ, "I love you. I know you. I know that you are the Alpha and the Omega. I know that you are eternal and that you are the Beginning and the End..."

I was so happy, dancing like a small child and praising God. Being a fair judge, God sentenced His Son to die in our place so we don't have to spend our eternity in Hell. We do not say that God Almighty has a son, from a wife – God forbid! We consider anyone infidel if they say so. God never had a wife or a physical son. We say that Christ is the Son of God in the same way light is born out of light. It is a spiritual son ship. We Egyptians are called 'sons of the Nile,' but we don't say that the Nile got married.

We proclaim in the Nicene Creed: "We believe... in one Lord Jesus Christ, the only begotten Son of God, begotten of His Father before all worlds, God of God, Light of Light, very God of very God, begotten, not made, being of one substance with the Father, by whom all things were made..." At the same time, we testify that there is no god but God, and we worship Him alone.

A few weeks later, I was baptized on September 6, 1987 at the house of a priest. In my heart, my baptism was my second date of birth. I have been a Christian over 20 years now. I told my wife that, when I die, I want my tombstone to read, "Christ is Victorious!"

All human beings on the face of this earth are mortal. Only Christ is immortal. All prophets are buried in tombs that we know and visit, but only the tomb of Christ is empty because He is in heaven, a Victorious King. Through His death on the cross,

Christ conquered the power of death. Praise and glory to you, my beloved Jesus!

A friend of mine stole my diary and gave it to Solomon of the Muslim brethren group. Solomon and his followers conspired together to trap me. They photocopied my diary, in which I explained my belief in Christ, and distributed it among the people in my village. It was like a scandal, but as Joseph said when his brothers conspired to harm him, "You intended to harm me, but God intended it for good" (Gen. 50:20). The Word of God says, "And we know that in all things God works for the good of those who love him" (Rom. 8:28).

My family members were ashamed of me. My mother could not appear in public. People used to point fingers at her because her son had brought her shame when he became a Christian. She told me that she had disowned me till the Last Day. Nothing broke my heart more than the hurt, humiliation and disgrace I caused my family, especially my mother. But what could I possibly do?

I really loved my mother, but it was impossible for me to abandon my belief in Christ for her. One day, she hit me on my head with her shoe. Another time, she wore black and announced to everyone that she was mourning the death of her son, Abraham.

One day all the people of my village came together to beat and torture me in order to convert me back to Islam. They kicked and slapped me in front of my family. My mother knelt down and begged them not to hurt me, but they stepped on her with their feet. My poor mother was crying on the ground, while they shouted at my family, "You disgraced us!" In the middle of this chaos, one of the village's Sheikhs shouted at the people, "What's the crime of this poor woman if her son has chosen the path of infidelity?" I thank the Lord. If it were not for His mercy, I would have been a martyr long ago.

Afterwards, all my friends avoided me. They thought I would give them a bad reputation in town. I became a famous 'guest' at the local police station and the State Security Investigations (SSI) office. I had to spend many nights at the police station in fear for my life. One night, the people in my village crowded around my family's house and wanted to burn it. They burned some of my Christian books, while the police confiscated the rest as if they were confiscating the property of a drug dealer.

The police had a 24-hour watch around my house to prevent any Christian material from coming to me. Well, the Word of God came to me in the form of a newspaper page that my sandwich was wrapped in! It was the front page of the newspaper, including an article by Pope Shenouda. He mentioned many Bible verses such as, *"Do not be afraid… for I am with you"* (Gen. 26:24), and *"The Lord himself goes before you and will be with you; He will never leave you nor forsake you. Do not be afraid; do not be discouraged"* (Due. 31:6-8)

It was a miracle and a sign from heaven to have this newspaper brought to me under the heavy siege of the police force surrounding my house. It encouraged and lifted me up at a time that I was in desperate need for God's help. As soon I finished reading that newspaper page, a police officer knocked on the door. Scared for my life, someone in my family snatched the paper and burned it. I was so sad to lose my source of consolation, but to my surprise the following day I was walking around the corner when I found another copy of the same page laying on the ground! I used to wake up every morning at 4 am to the voice of my mother crying to Allah to bring me back to Islam.

Christians are not dearer to me than my own mother. As a matter of fact, my mother is more precious to me than any Muslim or Christian. On the other hand, I had someone more precious than my mother or my very life – my Lord Jesus Christ! If I don't love Him more than myself I would not deserve to have a share with Him.

My mother left no stone unturned in order to get me back to Islam. She visited a sorcerer to cast a spell on me. Muslims think that the Jinn believe in the Qur'an. Well, there was nothing that sorcerer could do to affect me. I was praying to Almighty God in the name of Jesus Christ, the name that terrifies all demons and Jinn. Strangely enough, the sorcerer said to my mother, "Your son is following a path that he will never leave!"

God has done many signs and wonders in my life. I feel encouraged whenever I remember any of them. They are milestones along the way of God's fatherly love that carried me from the beginning and saw me through, and brought me to this place over 20 years ago. God has never forsaken me, not for a single moment!

Ibrahim

THE CHOSEN
ONES OF CHRIST

W hen we were little kids our father taught us how to pray. He was always committed to pray. My parents were simple people, but sincere in their worship and lifestyle. My father was a clerk and provided us with a reasonable living. I did not know much about my religion other than praying and wearing the veil. I was never concerned with Christianity or Christians. I thought it was forbidden to think of a religion that was corrupted.

I went to nursing school. After graduation, I worked at a private hospital, where I lived on the premises with some Christian nurses. For the first time in my life, I got in touch with Christians. Except for the few days I took off every month I lived with them. Contrary to my expectations, they treated me in a loving and friendly manner. I thought they would mistreat me since they were the majority at the hospital, and we Muslims were the minority.

I was attracted to these Christians. I started asking one of the doctors about little things that caught my attention, such as the picture of Christ on the cross. He answered all my questions, and I wanted to know more. He started giving me cassette tapes of sermons that explained so many things that I used to hear, but did not understand. I listened to these tapes secretly. Many things started to make sense. I noticed the character of Christ in the Qur'an and started looking for all the Qur'anic verses that spoke of Him.

I used to read these verses and meditate on their meaning. I found out that they attributed to Christ some characteristics that had never been attributed to a prophet – they were actually attributes of God. I felt as if I were reading these verses for the first time. My eyes were opened to a deeper meaning and significance in these verses other than the shallow explanation that I grew up believing.

I became further convinced and asked the doctor to explain the meaning of the Trinity and the Crucifixion. He answered all my questions. Everything he said pointed to the fact that Christ was really God, even the Qur'an gave that implication.

The doctor who had been my tutor traveled for a year, but I still continued to read and search. Everyday I became more convinced that Christ was God, until I found myself praying to Jesus and confessing Him as my Lord! One night, I was at the nurses' dorm lying on my bed, I was thinking of Christ and what I had to do to get baptized and change my religion. I wanted to live this new religion with all my heart, but I was afraid of what would happen to me if my family found out.

I got tired of thinking and decided to sleep. The room was dark, but suddenly I saw Christ standing on a vast meadow stretching His hand to me. I was drowning in a deep sea, surrounded by many people, none of them able to save me. I saw that vision three times in a row before I awoke. I was ecstatic. I kept shouting that I saw Him and that He appeared to me. When my friends asked me what had happened, I laughed but I told them nothing. That night was the happiest in my life. I was filled with a joy and peace that I had never experienced before.

I then faced a real crisis. I did not deny my faith and my family accused me of being insane. For three years they kept arranging for me to get married and I kept refusing. One time a man proposed to me, and my family insisted that I marry him. We were in the summer resort of Alexandria, playing on the beach, when my father and my brother took me into the sea. They tried to drown me. I cried and asked them why they did that. They said, "We won't kill you, but we wanted to show you that we can if you don't come to your senses and marry that man."

I lied to them and told them I would marry the man. I got engaged and went back to my job at the hospital. I'm sure things will change. I stopped contacting my family and I don't know what will happen next. I only know that I love Christ and live for Him, whatever troubles I may face.

Fatma

From Nominal Christianity to Islam

AND THEN TO CHRIST

We are all affected by our childhood and by our parents' lifestyle. I remember many things from my childhood as if they were yesterday – many painful memories. I witnessed so many bad arguments between my father and my mother. I had one sister and because of our parents' fights many nights we cried ourselves to sleep, without even having supper.

My father was a wealthy man and provided our family with a good living. We were Christians, who knew nothing about our Christianity. I can't remember my father or mother ever talking to us about God or Christianity. I know they never encouraged us to go to church.

I was an introvert with many psychological problems. As an adolescent, I decided to lead my own life my way, away from the stiffness of my family. Like me, my sister was rebellious and full of hate. She had many close friends and spent most of her time going out and having fun.

I decided to follow my sister's example. Whether good or bad I created my own world, my own relationships. From the time I was16 years old, I started smoking, drinking, partying and having affairs with women. I felt like a schizophrenic with two parts – the outward one having fun and getting drunk, the inward one sad and depressed. My dreams vanished and I felt miserable. Happiness was nothing but a few passing moments.

My sister and I grew apart even though we still loved each other. We shared the sadness, deprivation and tension of our home. We lost our relationship with God. I was never concerned about God. I never knew Him, and nobody told me about Him. My idea about God was that He had created us and left us alone. I believed that God lived in Heaven and did not interfere with our lives. He placed the right and the wrong before us, and one day He would use His authority to reward those who did good and punish those who did bad. My sister and I graduated from the university, but our lives were still the same. Many men proposed to my sister, but she always refused them categorically. My parents did not know the reason for her refusal and I really didn't care.

One day, I came home drunk at 3 am to find my parents in a very bad condition. I didn't pay much attention and tried to go to bed, but they shook me hard and woke me up in a very offensive way. After sobering up I understood that they were so upset because my sister had never come home. We looked for her. We even filed a missing-person's report at the police station, but it was all in vain. She vanished without a trace.

I felt so sad when my sister disappeared. Although our relationship was shallow, I loved her. She was my partner throughout the painful times we experienced but never talked about. My father and my mother were heartbroken. There were so many arguments and fights following her disappearance, each blaming the other of being the cause of it. They did not talk much about how they felt, but I could see it in their eyes.

After one month, my sister called us with a big surprise. She had gotten married to a Muslim man and had joined Islam herself! It got me thinking, "Who is God? What is the true religion? Why did my sister do that? What is the enticement of joining another religion?" I had so many questions tearing up my mind.

When my sister called a second time, my mother cried and my father begged her to come home. She told them that she was determined, that she had already changed her official papers and now had a Muslim name. She was also pregnant and wanted to raise her children as Muslims. I was surprised to hear that and wanted to meet her, so she gave me her new address.

I went to visit her and she welcomed me warmly like never before. Her husband welcomed me and was so friendly to me. I asked them about Islam and they started telling me about all the positive teachings in it. They tried to convince me that Christianity was infidelity and polytheism. I actually knew nothing about my own religion so could not compare and was very susceptible. They easily influenced me and I received all their ideas into my empty mind and ill soul. I told them that I was convinced, but needed some more time to think things over in order not to regret my decision afterwards.

I started thinking about the whole thing. I saw my sister happily following her new religion. I started wondering, "Is she really happy? Do the rituals of the new religion satisfy her? Does God respond to her prayers?" I was struggling with these thoughts. I had already made my decision, hoping to find God and myself through this new religion. I arranged for everything and prepared my papers.

Before I went to bed the phone rang. My mother answered and told me it was for me. When I said hello I heard music, Christian songs and a lady's voice, "Would you meet me now?" I was surprised and said, "Do you know me?" I certainly don't know her. "Who gave you my phone number? Why do you want to meet me?" Her response was that she wanted to pray with me.

By then I had already told my family and some of my friends that I was going to embrace Islam. I no longer feared the authority of my parents, the church or even God. I felt that I was following the 'true' God in Islam. My main concern was to save my soul after the empty life I had led before.

My friends tried so many times to talk with me, pray with me or take me to church. I refused bluntly and insisted that I was free to make my own decision. For some reason, this time things were different and with no hesitation, I told her to visit me and gave her my address. Fifteen minutes later the doorbell rang. After the usual introductions, she asked to pray with me. I was unusually quiet and agreeable. I didn't even ask her how she knew about me – I was silent and respectful in a very strange way. As she prayed I was crying my eyes out. She was asking the true God to stand beside me and guide me to make the right decision.

Her husband and their little daughter accompanied this lady. I was so amazed when the little girl looked at me and told me that she saw Jesus pouring water on me. They told me that Christ had baptized me and He loved me and still wanted me. They asked me to meet them in the morning to go to church because I had to start a personal relationship with Christ and learn everything about my religion. Then they left.

In the morning when they called I told them that I was not sure if I wanted to go. They came around anyway and took me to church. As we were entering the church, a lady came up to me and said, "I have to tell you something…" She seemed hesitant. She looked at me again and said, "Jesus says to you: I am the way, the truth and the life…" I broke down in tears. I was so overwhelmed with what was going on. I did not expect God to answer my questions in this way, telling me that Christ was the way, the truth and the life!

My life took a turn for the better. I started going to church regularly. I came to know God in a new way. I thought that God was far from me, but because He loved me, He came down to save me. I got away from all the bad things in my life like drinking and fornication. I started a new relationship with my father and my mother. I led them into a true relationship with God. Suddenly everything changed. We now go to church together and pray at

home. Arguments and fights are gone for good from our house
because God has touched each one of us. We pray fervently for
my sister, asking God to save her and bring her back.

Ashraf

THAT'S HOW I CAME TO KNOW GOD

*T*he best way to start my testimony is to thank God from the bottom of my heart. He has provided for a great conversion in my life and in the lives of all those who faithfully seek Him. God has led me with His mighty power and rescued me from the lion's den. Strangely enough, this conversion was not the result of a desire of mine, a reaction to something I heard or a sermon by a pastor or an evangelist. On the contrary, while I was running around attacking His Word and His people,

He had prepared everything to catch me with a net from which I could not escape! He is the Living God that seeks for the prodigal son. He stretches His hands to anyone who repents; He spreads His light to anyone who is lost in the world; He knocks softly on the door of every poor and ruined house to fill it with spiritual wealth, purity and holiness. He gives abundantly and does not regret doing so. He doesn't give us according to our actions, but according to His mercy.

I have been unwilling to write down my testimony because I was afraid to exaggerate. I did not want to be put on a pedestal. I don't deserve any of the credit. All glory belongs to God. I had also some pride left in me. I thought that proclaiming God's work in my life would be an insult to my ego, since I was the one who was cruel towards followers of the Living God – the same God who sought me and opened my eyes to see the light that I had never known before.

As you will read on the following pages, I had no choice but to surrender in this battle between a demon, who lived inside me, and a Holy God who offered me His salvation and opened His arms to hold me. I was really able to say with Job, "My ears had heard of you but now my eyes have seen you" (Job 42:5), and ask with David, "Create in me a pure heart, O God, and renew a steadfast spirit within me." (Ps. 51:10)

This is the Lord Jesus Christ, God's eternal Word and Spirit. He is the Way, the Truth and the Life; whoever believes in Him shall not die; whoever comes to Him shall not thirst or hunger;

He is the first and the last, the Alpha and the Omega, the Lord Jesus Christ!

My Life Before I Believed In Christ

I have to talk briefly about my life before I believed in Christ because it will show how much He loves us. Even while we are fighting against Him, He seeks us like a shepherd who searches for His sheep that has gotten lost in the wilderness.

I was born and raised in an extremely fundamental Muslim family. I followed their example with my free will, though perhaps my family influenced me. I started at the small 'Kottab' (Islamic learning place) that was in a remote area near our little village in Upper Egypt, 200 km South of Cairo.

In the beginning, my interests were focused on just memorizing the parts of the Qur'an that were part of our school curriculum. Gradually, my interest became more personal. I was motivated by my love for the words of God.

At that time, the Supreme Council of Islamic Affairs used to run an annual school competition in memorizing the Qur'an. All the schools of the Republic participated. My mother asked me to take part in it. So I did. I got the best grade and won first prize of

10 Egyptian Pounds. My father was happy to hear that and encouraged me to keep participating yearly in the competition just to get the financial award.

I continued to study the Qur'an diligently. I ended up memorizing more than 15 parts of the Qur'an before I finished prep school. I completed memorizing the whole Qur'an during high school. At that time, I used to live with my parents in the house with our extended family, including the rest of my uncles and cousins. One of my cousins was a fanatic Muslim. He was a student at El-Azhar Islamic University. He used to convince me to read books. There were times he would even buy me some books to read.

At one point, my immediate family moved into a separate house away from the extended family. My cousin traveled to an Arab country to work as an Islamic preacher in one of the mosques. He lived there for two years. When he came back, he told me that we did not know the true Islam through which we could go to "Al-Jannah" (heaven). He also told me that he had met with some of the Islamic leaders and Imams who managed to escape from the dictatorial ruler here. He asked me to go deeper in my studies of some books by the Imam Ibn Tammemah, Sheikh Sayed Kotb and Ibn Hazem Al-Zahery. In spite of the difficulty of some of those books, I still admired them. They proposed a path incredibly challenging for anyone to follow. For example, I found one of the Hadiths that said, "Whosoever would eat with or live with an infidel, becomes like him/her."

From that moment on, I was initiated into a new phase in my religious life. I began to examine people around me to know who was an infidel and who was a Muslim. I also started to gather the Qur'anic verses that would help me to differentiate between the true Muslims and the Non-Muslims; I wanted to delineate the nature of my relationship with each type. Eventually, I ended up in a very tense situation, discovering that my father, according to the criteria of that Hadith, was one of the infidels since he smoked and did not grow a beard. My mother did not pray; she used to call people names frequently. My brothers were also infidels since they would watch TV or smoke. Some of them did not perform the five daily prayers. Some of them did not grow a beard.

I was so upset with my brothers that I prevented them from continuing in certain phases of their studies. I also asked my father to divorce my mother since she did not obey me; this angered my father very much. I came to the final conclusion that my father, mother and brothers were all infidels. I asked my cousin whether I had to stay away from them, and he told me "Yes." I asked him if I ended my relationship with them, where would I go? He asked me to come and live with him.

"Do you have any doubts in your uncle and his wife regarding their faith?" he asked me. I said to him, "No, they are really true believers." He said, " So, come and bring all your belongings and live with me away from the life of infidelity and unfaithfulness in your house." So, I packed my luggage and left my family. With tears, my mother and brothers said good-bye to me. I didn't pity their tears, as I was fully determined not to be with infidels any more. I was beside myself with joy leaving my home for the sake of God.

My cousin settled in Cairo. He rented an apartment near El-Azhar University. He was in the final year of academic studies so I had to go back to my father's house in shame and humiliation. I asked my cousin, "Don't you think that my coming back to my father's house is a transgression?" He answered: "No, since necessity knows no law and need justifies the forbidden." He recited:

"But if one is forced by necessity, without willful disobedience, nor transgressing due limits, then is he guiltless. For Allah is oft-forgiving most merciful." (Surah 2:173)

I was on cloud nine, hearing that. I was in the final year of high school, and I decided to study hard so that no one would say that religion was an obstacle to academic success. I succeeded in earning high grades in the General Certificate of Education; I managed to join the Medical School, Cairo University.

Little by little, my mind was set free from all the patterns of thoughts that my cousin used to stress. I read many books he used to forbid by saying, "They carry thoughts of the Islamic Group 'Al-Takfeer and Al-Hijra' or the outlaws of the twentieth century. His words motivated me to go and discover what those people had to say.

In the medical school, I came across many political currents represented by small, legal groups. I made up my mind to join the religious group to keep the equilibrium with other groups. The group leader was a member of the faculty. He was also the general secretary. We had another man responsible for making contacts within the group members.

No doubt, I faced lots of difficulties inside the group. They led a traditional Islamic life that was far away from the right understanding of Islam in relationships with Non-Muslims (I do not mean Christians, but rather nominal Muslims). Thus, my religious ambitions grew more and more. I was frantic in my endeavor to reach a status like those who had adventures against the government and the regime. So, I started a nucleus, a small group. I taught them Islam, as I understood Islam to be. I felt their obedience and commitment. We used to pray together in a remote place away from mosques; since we came to the understanding that these were tantamount to what the Jews had built to hamper the Prophet Mohammad.

So, I started to sort out my relations with people according to their position and understanding of Islam. If anyone rejected what we said, he would be considered an infidel and would be treated like one,

> "Let not the believers take for friends or helpers unbelievers rather than believers." (Surah 3:28)

I had no difficulty doing that. All of us who were part of the group were driven by a great desire and enthusiasm to follow the example of the prophet Mohammed.

We always visualized Abu Obeida, son of Garah, described by the prophet Mohammed to be the nation's leader, killing his father when the latter refused to join Islam; Mosaab, son of Omair, who never listened to his mother's begging and left her to die because she rejected Islam; Abu Bakr, who told his father he would kill him if he did not join Islam. All these pictures made us crueler towards our families and our friends if they refused our version of Islam. It was painful to shout at my mother and my father, and to swear at my brothers and sisters, threatening to kill them, but my only motive was to obey Allah and the Prophet. I wanted to reach the status of those who obeyed God. I kept reminding myself of the Prophet Mohammed's Hadith, "Anyone of you has not become a true believer until he loves Allah and the Prophet more than his money, his children or even himself."

There was a sect of people with whom we needed to define our relationship according to the Qur'an and Sunnah. It was People of the Book, and Christians in particular since no Jews lived in Egypt; even if some of them lived there, they had no relationship with anybody. After searching the Prophet Mohammed's attitude towards Christians, we found the picture was very dark. However, it was fine with us since we were jealous of their simplicity, courtesy and their remarkable sociability with nominal Muslims. They had a strange kind of calmness in the face of all the hassles and assaults we caused them. We interpreted that as a dirty attempt on their part to get out of their seclusion as a minority among a Muslim majority. We reasoned that the only thing they could do was to cunningly and maliciously treat Muslims nicely; otherwise, they would have no place among us. That's exactly what the Qur'an said about them.

"They were covered with humiliation and misery: they drew on themselves the wrath of Allah." (Surah 2:61)

Our hatred towards Christians took the form of harassment and assaults against them on the streets, but they answered our assaults with disgusting meekness. We responded by being more aggressive against them, and we started to plan how we could torture and intimidate them. We learned that God had legalized killing them, plundering their possessions and looting their houses. According to the Qur'an, all their belongings were to be considered "a gift" from God to the Muslims.

"What Allah has bestowed on His Messenger and taken away from the people of the townships, belongs to Allah, to His Messenger." (Surah 59:7)

It means that all their belongings are to be taken from them without war just as the Prophet did with the Jews of Bani Kuraizah when he encircled them, killed their young men, took captive their women and occupied their land with all the palm trees and kicked them out of their city.

Although we could not do what the Prophet did, we managed to break into the shops of the Christians and rob them. The enmity and hatred in our hearts reached the peak when we attacked their churches in different parts of the village where I used to live. The top of operations was the plan to attack and destroy one of the churches. This attack disturbed the government when the Coptic Christians demonstrated against that incident. At the same time, the government seemed to be happy about that incident since they treated us very well in prison.

After we served our sentence, the villagers received us like heroes. This was a good motivation for us to go on persecuting the Christians, but with more wisdom and prudence to avoid being arrested by the police. All these events took place in such a short time. I got more involved and the news went on like wild fire among my fellow students. As a result, one of the top leaders of the Islamic Group called "El-Takfeer wal-Hijrah" wanted to sit with me to express his deep thanks and appreciation for my distinguished courage and love to God and His Prophet. I knew that he belonged to Shukri's group and I became so happy about that. I wanted to be one of them. That leader was very careful in his conversation with me. In one of the summer vacations we arranged a camp for the Medical School's Islamic Group. We got the financial support for that camp from the school's administration. The goal of that camp was to spend much time discussing concepts of Islam.

After the camp, my friend asked me my viewpoint regarding the Islamic Group and wondered if I would like to join them if I got the chance. He kept on quoting from Hadith's about the necessity of joining a group following God, His Sunnah and His Prophet. One statement was, "He who dies without having a fealty, dies like a Pre-Islamic infidel." He also said, "There is no Islam without a group; no group without an Emir."

I felt, since I loved God and the Prophet, that the best thing to do was to join the Islamic Group. This particular group was the closest to my idea about Islam. They arranged for me to meet the group's Emir at the house of a member in Cairo. I shook Emir Shokry's hand and said to him, "I commit to you to hear and obey, through thick and thin, and to put you ahead of myself, unless I witness public infidelity from you." Fealty was not just words you repeat; you practically put your life in the hands of the Emir. You would sell yourself to God and the Prophet.

I was so ecstatic that day; the only time I was happier was the day I got baptized later. Fealty made me submit to the Emir without any fear. I did anything he wanted without even thinking of the pain and struggles I would face because I felt I was obeying God and the Prophet. I was ready to do even more than I was asked. I started to treat my family harshly. I stopped greeting them. When they questioned me I would recite to them,

> "Shall we tell you of those who lost most in respect of their deeds? Those whose efforts have been wasted in this life, while they thought that they were acquiring good by their works?" (Surah 18:103).

My father asked me to tell him what, in my opinion, would make him a real Muslim. I told him to grow his beard and not to listen to the radio. He agreed. I then said to him, "My mother does not pray; therefore, she is an infidel and you cannot live with her." My father was outraged. He shaved his beard and almost hit me with a big stone, but I ran away.

I have to say that the first thing that motivated me to join the Islamic Group was that they were so hostile towards Christians, whom I hated very much. I always searched for Qur'anic verses to justify my hatred and give me a clear conscience for what I did.

Shokry appointed me an Emir for a smaller group in a Cairo suburb. He was so proud of me and of my commitment to the cause. He called me 'Abu Obeida.' Each one of the group members had a nickname; we never knew each other's real names.

Shokry trusted me more and more. He sent me to some Arab and foreign countries to make contact with members of the group. We cooperated together to attract new members to join the group and receive their fealty on behalf of Emir Shokry Mustafa.

The government was hassling us; therefore, we had to escape for a short time to the hills outside Menia, Badary and Assiut. Every time we got arrested, we were sent to Cairo and then released. We all felt the necessity of changing location because we could no longer live among the infidels, according to the Prophet's Hadith, "I reject anyone who lives among infidels." We had to send a member to check out the best place to 'emigrate' to. We were looking for a permanent place to live, coming back only to execute judgment on the secular regime that did not follow God's commandment.

One day in 1977, another member and I were ordered to look for a furnished apartment in a poor, highly populated area, no questions asked. We found a suitable apartment and we rented it, still not knowing why. The following day we knew that Sheikh Mohammed had been kidnapped by some of our members. A few minutes later, another member visited us and told us the whole story. Sheikh Mohammed always attacked our group. To be honest, he used to write false things about us, stating we would marry one woman to more than one man. Our group warned him many times to stop these attacks, but he took it lightly.

We were told that the purpose of that operation was to put more pressure on the government in order to release some of the leaders who had been arrested in connection with the incident of the Military Technical Academy. Our group also wanted to ask for a money ransom to cover some of our many expenses.

A few hours later, most, if not all members of our group were arrested all over Egypt. Even people who just had a distant relation to our group were arrested as well. We were transferred to the Kalla Jail where we spent two years of being tortured and questioned in what was labeled 'the case of belonging to an anti-government group.' Two years later, we were released. We had to leave the country as soon as possible. We divided ourselves and scattered in some Arab countries, waiting for orders from the Emir, whom Shokry had appointed to fill his place. That was the beginning of the end for the group. I can honestly say that if it weren't for the 'Sheikh Mohammed Operation,' our group would have had great power in running things in Egypt.

As I mentioned before, some of us were looking for a town to which we could emigrate in preparation for the great Jihad. We were told that the place was found, and many brothers already went there. At the beginning of 1980, I joined the rest of the group at that area. It was a desert area with nobody around, with the exception of some Bedouins who passed through. We prepared a place to stay and started moving in small groups, since we had only one car. Many of our members had grown up in this area so they helped us a great deal to get to know the terrain and the traditions of this new community. We managed to dig some water wells in our camp. We had a secret password to get in and out. We took turns guarding the camp. We trained in shooting weapons and provided everyone with a rifle to defend themselves in case of an attack.

For the first few days, things went fine and we were happy. We remembered the time when the Prophet Mohammed immigrated to Medina. We looked forward to the day we would go back to Egypt and conquer it as the Prophet did Mecca. We had a tradition that each one of us, having left his infidel family and emigrated for the sake of God, would repeat the following poetic stanza:

Good-bye, my homeland; it might be a long time!

Your people and mine have abandoned God's Book!

It's hard for me to leave, but I'm seeking the Truth!

We repeated these words with full enthusiasm. We cared for nothing but the Islamic call. We were ready to face all difficulties for the sake of God. We thought if we died we would go to heaven; otherwise we would win the battle. This poetic stanza filled us with joy and pride, but filled our eyes with tears and sadness, missing our friends and families.

The town that we immigrated to experienced trouble, unrest and guerrilla warfare. All the town's people were armed, which made it easier for us to carry weapons hassle free. The local authorities got wind of our presence through the Bedouins, who sometimes got lost in the desert in our area and came to us to ask the way back. One day, through his telescope one of our guards observed two armed cars coming towards our camp. When they were a few meters away, he stopped them and asked them what they wanted. They wanted to meet us to find out who we were and what group we belonged to. They also wanted to know why we were in this area. They were concerned that we belonged to the dissidents of that area. After a long conversation, in which I took part, they discovered that we were not locals but newcomers to the area. This made them more suspicious. After a lot of discussions, they made it clear that we had to leave the camp and abandon our dream in that area.

Since we were in a country next to Egypt, going back was easy and didn't cost us a lot of money. Even though we all decided to go back to Cairo, some of us, for some unforeseeable reason decided to stay for a long time. During that period, we got to know some brothers who participated in the Afghanistan war. We managed to convince them that the Afghanistan war was not for the sake of God and Islam. They proclaimed fealty (loyalty) to our group and helped us a lot until we went back to Egypt by the beginning of 1990.

As we approached Cairo, we were arrested and taken to the Ministry of Interior. After a time of questioning, they released us.

We tried, together with those who remained faithful, to rebuild the group. We used to meet twice a month to study and reformulate the main ideas of the group. This task was completed by February 1990.

One day, one of our brothers, whose task was to review books, magazines and newspapers, gathering information about similar Islamic groups all over the world. He came to us, upset. He asked us, "Have you read the papers today?" We said, "No, what's the matter?" He said, "They arrested a group of missionaries who converted nominal Muslims to Christianity by alluring them with money or involving them in sexual relationships." Since it was the Holy month of Ramadan, we were so ashamed. We had to take a stand against evil. But how? By hand? That would be difficult. By words? That would be the least we could do, but how and when?

THE BEGINNING

When we read that newspaper, we felt humiliated that we fell short of standing for God. We decided to play an aggressive role against Christian evangelism in order to stop them at any cost. After long arguments, we ruled out the military solution for many reasons. You see the state security system had improved in Egypt way beyond where it used to be in the 1970s. The active leaders of our group, who managed to sneak any brother in danger outside the country, were gone and we had no replacements. Some of those leaders had been executed; others were serving life sentences.

Therefore, we excluded the military option and searched for another way to counteract Christian evangelism. Finally, we thought of the 'logical confrontation' – expose the false teachings and corruption in the Torah and the Bible. All the leaders hailed that approach. Now we started looking for the person who would assume this great responsibility of highlighting the truth and defeating the infidels. I never expected to be a candidate for that task, not for lack of ability, but because everyone knew how much I hated Christians. After a long time of tense silence, the voice of the Emir announced the name of the person chosen to do that job. I almost fainted when I heard my name. I was beside myself with anger. How could they ask me to do that job, one that entailed, of course, reading Jewish and Christian books?

Our Emir looked at me and said, "This is an order! You have no choice but to comply if you really believe in Allah and the Last Day." He quoted from the Qur'an:

> "It is not fitting for a believer, a man or a woman, when a matter has been decided by Allah and His Messenger, to have any option about their decision." (Surah 33:36)

I tried to convince the Emir to choose someone else, but he refused. He said to me, "I feel that you're the best man for this task.

If you do it well you will kill two birds with one stone. First, you will educate all Muslims and open their eyes to the facts they can't see. Second, you will earn a lot of 'good' money, because your research will be translated and published all over the world."

His words made me anxious to get to the research. The Emir said, "Your research should have two parts: first, to prove from the Torah and the Bible the authenticity of Mohammed's call as a prophet, as the Qur'an says:

"Those who follow the Messenger, the unlettered Prophet, whom they find mentioned in their own (Scriptures), in the Taurat (Torah) and the Gospel" (Surah 7:157);

Second, to prove, by finding contradictions, that the Torah and the Bible that people have today are not the same Books inspired by God; they were altered and corrupted."

Unwillingly, I accepted the mission. I said to the Emir, "But this task necessitates that I buy a Torah and a Bible to read." He told me that we would go downtown Cairo to buy them. We walked on Gomhoria Street until we found a bookstore that sold these books. We could not walk into the bookstore wearing our traditional outfit because it was so conspicuous. The people at the bookstore would probably call the police thinking that we came to wreck it. A man was passing by and we stopped him and asked him his name. We asked him to go into the bookstore and buy the book for us. He did.

The Emir and I then went to my house in south Cairo, which took more than a two hours, during which time I tried my best to get rid of the Bible. Once I left it on a seat; another time I pretended I forgot it, but each time the Emir would bring it to me and remind me to keep it with me. Finally, we made it home and the Emir departed for his hometown and left me to start my unwilling journey with the Torah and the Bible.

The first day was the most difficult. I was under the impression that the Bible was not from God, and that it might bring demons into my house and I wouldn't be able to pray. To be safe I kept it outside my bedroom. For many days I was paranoid. Whenever I heard a sound at the house, I thought God had sent demons to punish me for having this book. I did not keep the Bible in the room where I prayed because I thought the angels would not come into the room if it were there.

I had these fears for a long time until I realized that I did not choose to have this book at my house. I just obeyed God, through obeying the Emir. The prophet Mohammed commanded us in his Hadith to obey the Emir, "Whoever obeyed my Emir has obeyed me, and whoever disobeys my Emir has disobeyed me." I came to the conclusion that I was carrying out the orders of the God-appointed Emir and, therefore, the Bible would not harm me if I kept it in my room; Allah would help me.

The group provided me with everything I needed. They gave me 500 Egyptian pounds every month as an allowance in return for my full time research. Every time I tried to forget about that research, I would remember the Hadith, "Whoever obeys my Emir has obeyed me, and whoever disobeys my Emir has disobeyed me." I would ask God for forgiveness three times and then pray. Nothing distracted me from doing that job. I had many references that helped me do my best, and I already had a good knowledge of Christian issues. So, I made the decision to start this difficult journey.

I was worried because I did not know where or how to start. I did not have a specific method to approach the two parts of the research. For example, regarding the issue of proving Mohammed's prophethood, I expected to find the exact name 'Mohammed' in the Torah and the Bible, or at least 'Ahmed' or 'Mahmoud.' I did not know where or how to start. Things were muddled up in my mind. I was not sure which name I should look for in the Torah: Mohammed? Ahmed? Mahmoud?

I got really confused, so I decided to move to the second part of my research, and to look for differences and contradictions in order to prove that the Torah and the Bible were not from God. Likewise, I failed to define a standard by which I could measure the Torah and the Bible and refute them. I was upset because these things, somehow, made me feel inept in doing this research. Giving in was not one of my qualities, so I decided to focus and save no effort to achieve my goal.

The Emir and I met once a month to discuss the research. Every time I asked him to change his mind and assign it to someone else that I could assist. However, he would strangely insist that I was the one for that job.

I prayed and asked God for strength. I felt unusually brave and started to read the Bible, but without any system or method. I started with the book of Genesis and I did not know what I was supposed to look for. I found strange names that I had never heard before in my life, which made me upset. I threw the book in the corner and said angrily, "Those Jews and Christians are stupid. How could they say that such a strange book, full of strange names, is from God? They are crazy!" I stopped reading.

Two days later, I went back to reading the Bible. This time I did not read in Genesis because I did not want to come across those difficult names and words. I flipped some pages and continued reading. I was impressed by the writings in the books of Numbers, Exodus and Deuteronomy. I found a lot of information about Moses, Pharaoh and the Israelites, written in detail, which satisfied my curiosity.

I finished reading the Old Testament in two months, but it was a superficial reading, nothing in depth. I read it once again, this time looking for anything relevant to Mohammed, Ahmed or Mahmoud, but found nothing. I moved to reading the New Testament. I read it completely, but did not reach any conclusions since I could not understand the whole thing. I felt angry with the Emir who got me caught up in this research from the beginning.

When the Emir visited me I told him that I could not find any clue that could lead me to what we were looking for. I had read the Torah and the Bible and did not find anything. The Emir told me that there was a book that we used to study abroad that would help me a great deal in my research. It was called *'Revealing the Truth,'* written by the late Sheikh El-Hindi. I looked for that book in my personal library until I found it.

'*Revealing the Truth*' was a valuable reference for us, especially when we debated with Christians to convince them that Islam was the true religion. It contained erroneous quotations from the Torah and the Bible, which we used to tell Christians who converted to Islam. We used it successfully with three people in a row.

I started a new way of research, with the help of some other books that the Emir gave me, such as *Sects and Denominations* by Shahristani, Deciding on Sects and Cults by Ibn Hazm, and some other historical and biographical writings that attacked Christianity. I wrote down all the verses that Ibn Hazm said were contradictory and looked them up in the Torah and the Bible. Most of the verses I found were phrased differently, or referred to some different people. I did find many verses that had some contradictions, but if we used these verses as basis to prove that the Torah was not authentic, we would have to accept similar verses in the Qur'an, and that, too, would be not from God. (I later wrote down my findings in a research paper titled, *In Reply to Ibn Hazm*).

I searched sincerely, motivated only by my love toward God and the Prophet. My group noticed my increasing fascination with the Bible. They always asked me about it and I always lied to them. I had to make up an excuse, so I told them that we were meeting some Christian young people to invite them to Islam and we had to know their background.

After failing in my attempts to undermine the Torah by proving its contradictions, I decided to try the second part of my assignment, i.e. to establish from the verses of the Torah and the Bible that Mohammed was the Messenger of God. I looked into

El-Hindi's book, *Revealing the Truth,* and I was ecstatic to find what I desired. I joyfully prayed and thanked God that He had led me to these verses. I started to write them down in the following order:

Gen. 17:20	Gen. 49:10	Deut. 18:18-20	Deut. 32:21
Deut. 33:1-3	Isa 42:9	Isa 54: 1-3	Isa 65: 1-2
Ps. 45: 1-3	Ps. 149:3	Dan 2: 31-32	Matt. 3:2
Matt. 13:31	Matt. 20:1	Matt. 21:33	John. 14:15
Rev. 2:27			

These were not the only verses that El-Hindi mentioned to prove Mohammed's prophethood. There were some other verses, which I excluded because they were not as clear. I studied these verses very carefully and objectively. We, as a unique group of believers, never accepted any information without a strong proof from a reliable source. These verses were, on the surface, very appealing to any Muslim to accept, but through scrutinizing – the method of fundamental Muslims – one would find that the deduction based on the proof was invalid.

Therefore, I collected all the books that I thought would help me in my research. I started to imagine my future after the success of my research. I would have done God and the Prophet a great favor and gained a handsome amount of money. Speaking of money, the Emir and I went to the Sunnah Advocates bookstore and explained to them the idea of my book. They were impressed. They asked for one chapter as a sample and offered to buy its copyright. I dreamed of becoming rich and famous because of the book I was to write, but my main motivation was to proclaim victory for Islam.

I started reading the Bible once again. I became an addict of Bible reading. I wrote many evidences to prove, with logic and corroboration, that the Torah and the Bible confirmed Mohammed's prophethood. The outcome was not good. For the sake of absolute confirmation of Mohammed's divine message I was meticulous in my research. I depended on many references, such as *The Dictionary of Countries* by Yakot El-Hamawi. I came across a town named Faran. I checked it out to see where it was and what its modern name was. I also used linguistic dictionaries such as *Arabs' Tongue* and even Hebrew dictionaries to understand meanings of words like 'Shelon,' for example.

I wanted to produce a book that not one person could refute, not even one word of it. Unfortunately, things did not go the way I had planned. All my logic and linguistic deductions fell one after the other. I could not find a single verse that emphasized my theory. (By the way, I wrote another booklet called, *'The Stifled Truth,'* in which I mentioned all the verses that I studied and how I reached a conclusion that they did not refer to the Prophet Mohammed).

I finished studying all these verses, but did not find what I was looking for. My feelings were a mixture of sadness, despair, anxiety and confusion. It never crossed my mind that Mohammed was not a prophet. I tried to soothe myself with the conclusion that I failed to connect the evidence to the character of the Prophet.

I decided to give the matter another try. This time I used other books, such as *Evidences of Prophethood, Dictionary of Countries,* and *The Arabic Encyclopedia.* I tried my best not to fail this time. Failure, after all the trouble I had been through, meant destruction of my whole life. Well, the second time was no better than the first, but even worse! The second time I came across many points that opposed my theory.

Sometimes, I would look at the huge number of Islamic books and references and wonder, "Could it be possible that all these books have deceived us and presented us with an imaginary character? If that was the case, God would not deserve to be worshipped." I would not go down this path. Then I would quickly pray and ask God for forgiveness.

All of a sudden, I found myself overlooking the subject of my research and going back to reading the Bible for the third time. I found a strange delight in reading the Bible, so much so that I feared I was falling under a spell. We used to say that Christians were sorcerers who derived their magic from the Torah and the Bible. Nevertheless, the Bible attracted me in a strange, irresistible way.

The Emir visited me regularly. Every time I expected him to be upset with me for not achieving my goal and to relieve me of my assignment. On the contrary, every time he seemed more enthusiastic than before, assuring me that I was the best one for that job.

I started reading the Gospel of Matthew and already stumbled even before I finished the first chapter. I saw that they traced the genealogy of Christ back to David. I thought they were crazy.

I consoled myself with the thought of finding what I was look-ing for. I was really fascinated by chapters four, five and six of the Gospel of Matthew. I had read that part twice before, but this time it was like I was reading it for the first time in my life. I felt as if there was a hand tapping my head and opening my mind. I heard a voice inside me saying, "It's about time you understood what you're reading without being concerned about who's right and who's wrong." I was shivering for no apparent reason, and felt as if I was in a semi-trance.

I found the Bible speaking about what we did with Christians as if it recorded the present events. I read what the Bible said about persecution, humiliation and murder – our idea of obeying God. "How strange that this Bible knew what we said and did to Christians! Could it be that Christians recently added that part?"

We always interpreted Christians' love and humility as fear of us Muslims because they were a weak minority; as the Qur'an put it:

"They were covered with humiliation and misery." (Surah 2: 61).

I found many verses promoting love, obedience, submis-sion and even love towards enemies. I was puzzled, "How could someone write down the cause of his own humiliation?"

Whenever I read God's commandment for Christians to love their enemies, I remembered my harsh treatment of my parents. I was too cruel to them. I always found new ways to hurt them. One time, I got ill and underwent a serious surgery at a hospital.

My father wanted to see me, but I refused and said that I did not want to see an infidel. My mother used to send me food through a third party; otherwise I would refuse to accept it. She used to stand for hours outside my hospital window, in the scorching heat, just to steal a look at me through the window.

These memories always made me cry and curse the day I knew Allah. I used to console myself by thinking of what Abu Obeida, son of Garah, and Abu Bakr El-Sedeek did to their own fathers; and Mosaab, son of Omira, to his mother. That would calm down my feelings.

I finished reading the Gospel of Matthew, but its words were carved in my memory. They chased me day and night, and whenever I wanted to do something bad, I read the rest of the Gospels and the Epistles and was amazed to find philosophy and rhetoric superior to those of the Qur'an. Since the Bible was written 630 years before Islam, how could we say that the Qur'an was unique in rhetoric?

One chilly winter night, I was reciting a Surah from the Qur'an, hoping to erase the words of the Gospel of Matthew from my mind. The brothers and I were jealous, always envying Christians because they enjoyed close friendships with many people. In contrast, we could not establish even casual relationships with minimum tolerance, so as to invite people to join Islam. This was a great obstacle in our way. The Islamic call did not permit us any leeway for building relationships that would bring us closer to people – the very thing we needed in order to attract them to Islam.

Our life was full of violence, cruelty and terrorism. This was not our normal behavior. We felt that if we did not act this way, we would not be obedient to Allah. Allah had stated in the Qur'an the way we were to treat the infidels, whether People of the Book, polytheists or false Muslims. The Qur'an says about People of the Book:

"O, ye, who believe! Take not the Jews and the Christians for your friends and protectors: they are but friends and protectors to each other. And he amongst you that turns to them (for friendship) is of them. Verily Allah guideth not a people unjust." (Surah 5:51)

As for the other kinds of infidels, such as Muslims who did not pray, tithe, grow beards or commit a sin and refuse to repent, the Qur'an says:

"O ye who believe! Take not for friends unbelievers rather than believers." (Surah 4:144)

As for family members and relatives, the Qur'an states:

"O ye who believe! Take not for protectors your fathers and your mothers if they love infidelity above Faith: if any of you do so, they do wrong." (Surah 9:23)

"Thou wilt not find any people who believe in Allah and the Last Day loving those who oppose Allah and His Messenger, even though they were their fathers, or their sons, or their brothers, or their kindred." (Surah 58:22)

If we add to these Qur'anic verses the authentic Hadith told by El-Bokhary by Muslim and by El-Termezy; according to Omar, the Prophet Mohammed said, "Do not shake hands with People of the Book; do not return their greetings; if they meet you on the road, push them off the side."

There were scores of these verses that defined our relationship with our families, friends and non-Muslims. We had no say in defining these relations because of Islamic thinking in general, and the Qur'an in particular, did not give the Muslim any room to use his mind. On the contrary, anyone who used his mind to explain a verse or a Hadith would be labeled 'infidel.' You had to accept things as Mohammed interpreted them. If there was something that Mohammed did not mention, you were to stay away from it. El-Bokhary mentioned a Hadith. According to Ibn Abbass, the Prophet Mohammed said, "Whoever expressed his own opinion of the Qur'an, would have reserved his place in Hell."

After all these Qur'anic verses and Hadiths, how could we be nice or friendly towards those who differ from us? We could not do that, as the Qur'an says:

"And incline not to those who do wrong, or the Fire will touch you." (Surah 11:113)

My heart was filled with anger and resentment whenever I read in the Bible verses that talked about love and forgiveness.

Many times I felt ashamed while reading the Bible that we claimed to be corrupted. I wondered if Christians altered the Bible and still gained people's love and respect, how did we, who did not alter God's word, fail in that? Something had to be wrong.

I tried to brush aside these thoughts. A thought kept coming back. What if I did not reach a conclusion in my research? I was struggling so much that every time I had these thoughts I cried out loud, "May God forgive me. I proclaim that there is no God but Allah and Mohammed is His Messenger." I would then rush to pray to get rid of these thoughts. I told myself that Mohammed was actually the Messenger of Allah, even if I could not prove it from the Torah and the Bible.

My problem became more serious. Instead of looking for evidence to prove Mohammed's prophethood, I found myself attracted by the sweet words of the Torah and the Bible. I wondered, "How can I get rid of their influence on me?" "How can I prove that the Torah and the Bible were not from God? All the ideas recorded in them both were good and could not have been written by man. How could people penetrate the depths of the future and talk, two thousand years ago, about things happening in the present time? If we assumed, for the sake of argument, that man compiled the Torah and the Bible, we would have put man on the same level with God in knowledge and wisdom. We certainly know that God is omniscient and omnipotent.

I suddenly found myself reading the Book of Psalms, and then the Book of Proverbs. I learned some verses from Psalms 23 and 143 and repeated them in my prayers. Anyone who heard me praying was touched by these verses and would ask me to write them down so they could use them in prayer. I still tried to find evidences of Mohammed's prophethood and the Bible's fallibility, but could not find anything. I struggled with doubts and conflicting thoughts inside me. I tried to ignore them, but they were growing stronger every day. I loved God, but my background and my love of my religion always prevented me from thinking that Islam might not be the true religion given by God. I became confused and restless. I could not enjoy a good night's sleep like before.

One time I was praying at dawn. While reciting the Qur'an I suddenly stopped and my mind wandered. I asked myself, "What would you do if, for example, Islam turned out not to be the way to heaven?" I tried to brush aside this question, but I could not. I could not even finish the dawn prayer. I cried my eyes out until I fell asleep on the carpet. A couple of hours later, my mother woke me up. I went to work absent-minded. I did not know where I was walking or to whom I was talking.

When I came back home, I felt a strong desire to read the Bible. I read the Gospel of John, chapters one to fifteen. I found the highest kind of rhetoric, philosophy and linguistic expressions that were very elegant and cohesive – especially when the Bible talks about the sheep and the shepherd; the vine and the gardener; the branches that bear fruit and those that do not they are thrown into the fire.

I screamed at the top of my voice, "Oh, God, have mercy on your servant! Please tell me where you are and on which side: are you with the Jews and Christians? Or Muslims? Please have

mercy on me. I am your servant. I committed my life to follow
you. I am grateful for all your favors. I cannot stand before you,
and you would not step down to stand before a breath of yours.
You are Almighty God and I am the helpless human being who
cannot do anything until you allow me to. You are the Most Merciful, Most Compassionate and I am your servant with no power
or wisdom. My whole life is in your hand. I have loved you since
childhood. I sacrificed myself for the sake of heaven and your
love. I did not care about prison or torture – even the whole world
could not stand in my way of my seeking you. Why do you treat
me this way? I loved you and tried to please you the way your
Prophet Mohammed taught us, but here I am – helpless and unable to continue. Each side says that you are their God. I don't
know who's right and who's wrong. Oh, God, shall I swear to
you that I love you? I think not, because you know everything.
Oh, how much I suffered in my search for you! I left my studies,
my family and my friends. I wandered like a stranger. I was imprisoned and tortured for your sake. Why didn't you answer me?
If you are the God of Muslims, take out everything from my mind
except Islam, and if you are the God of Christians, give me some
light to follow."

I hardly slept and my mind was spinning: "What if Islam is
not God's way? What if God's way is the Torah and the Bible?
Are you going to follow Christians?" I would shiver thinking of
what could happen to me, as if God and people would blame me.
One day, I brushed aside all my fears and told myself, "What do
you want? Enough is enough! You are no longer as you used to

be. You have two ways before you, and both seem straight. Don't waste your time and look for God's way with all your strength. It doesn't matter if it is the Jews, Christians or Muslims; the only important thing if that it would be God's way – that is, if you really search for God. This is your destiny and you have to accept it. Be sure that God will respond to you according to your sincerity. Forget that you are a Muslim and start searching afresh. What would prevent you?"

I thought about it and said, "Oh, God, please lead my steps and give me strength because I'm facing a hard trial. If you don't help me, demons will tear me up. I will wander the earth, aimless and restless. Oh, God, please help me. I promise to follow you wherever you are, even with the Christians, whom I can't stand." I suddenly felt a certain peace and tranquility overwhelming my whole being. For the first time I was thinking logically.

I reached a conclusion: Christians went astray and became infidels for two reasons. First, they said that the Christ, Isa, son of Mary, was God; second, they said that he died on the cross and rose to redeem people from their sins. Why don't I focus my research on these two issues and examine them from an Islamic point of view? I was curious to know what the Islamic scholars thought of these issues.

I started going through books of Islamic history, biography and exegesis. I looked for anything related to Christ and whether he manifested God's attributes as mentioned in the Qur'an. I used reliable and authentic references like *The Interpretation* by Ibn Kathir, *History of Islam* by Dhahabi, *Beginning and End* by Ibn

Kathir, *Sects and Denominations* by Sherhristani, *Deciding on Sects and Cults* by Ibn Hazm (also known as Abu Mohammed), *Holy Books before Islam*, and *Christianity between Logic and Recount*. As a result of my intensive research, I found some attributes of Christ that even Christians did not deal with in their books. For example:

1) The Ability to Create:

The Qur'an says:

"That is Allah, your Lord! There is no god but He, the Creator of all things." (Surah 6:102)

"For verily it is thy Lord who is the All-Creator, knowing all things." (Surah 15:86)

"Those on whom, besides Allah, ye call, cannot create (even) a fly, if they all met together for the purpose." (Surah 22:73)

"Those whom they invoke besides Allah create nothing and are themselves created." (Surah 16:20)

"Is then he who creates like one that creates not?" (Surah 16:17)

These are but some of the verses that restrict the ability to create to God only. When God wanted to distinguish Himself from other gods, He highlighted this attribute of His that surpassed all other gods. Meanwhile, the Qur'an clearly admits that Christ created things:

"I make for you out of clay, as it were, the figure of a bird, and breathe into it, and it becomes a bird by Allah's leave." (Surah 3:49)

"Thou makest out of clay, as it were, the figure of a bird, by my leave, and thou breathest into it, and it becometh a bird by my leave." (Surah 5:110)

When I read these verses I thought in my heart: it was God who gave Christ this ability; it was not part of his essence even though, Christ was the only one on whom God bestowed one of His divine attributes. Why Christ and not Mohammed? God said to Mohammed:

"Canst thou cause the deaf to hear the call?" (Surah 27:80),

Which is a lot easier than creation. God did not give Mohammed, the best of His people and the Seal of the Prophets, the ability to make the deaf hear. He challenged people to create a fly, but gave Christ the ability to create birds. Birds are small creatures, but it is not a matter of size, but of principle. He who creates a small creature can create a big one. This cannot be of man, but of God.

2) Knowing What is Hidden:

God spoke of Himself in the Qur'an:

"Say: none in the heaven or on earth, except Allah, knows what is hidden." (Surah 27:65),

"With Him are the keys to the unseen, the treasures that none knoweth but He." (Surah 6:59).

In the first verse, the Qur'an emphasizes beyond any doubt that knowing what is hidden belongs only to God and nobody else. The second verse underlines the fact that only God knows the unseen and the future.

Meanwhile, the Qur'an teaches about Mohammed that he used to rebuke anyone who attributed to him the ability to know what was hidden:

"Say: I tell you not that with me are the treasures of Allah, nor do I know what is hidden." (Surah 6:50).

One time Moaz said to Mohammed, "… if Allah wills and you will," and Mohammed interrupted him saying, "How could you make me equivalent to Allah? No one in heaven or on earth knows what is hidden but Allah."

As for Christ, we find all limitations removed. He knows and does what every other person cannot. The Qur'an says:

"And I declare to you what ye eat, and what ye store in your houses." (Surah 3:49)

It is very unusual that in these verses Christ speaks in the first person; it must be God himself speaking. On the other hand, Mohammed was always told what to 'say.' Christ was unique because he spoke of himself, which means that his abilities were His and not acquired.

In *Beginning and End* by Ibn Kathir, part two and page 86, I read a story that made me ashamed. It was a proof beyond any doubt that Christ possessed supernatural powers to know what was hidden. (It is a long story; those interested may refer to the book by Ibn Kathir).

3) Healing the Sick:

The Qur'an mentions Abraham's words that God is the only healer:

"And when I am ill, it is He who cures me." (Surah 26:80)

Mohammed said in an authentic Hadith, "Oh, Allah, there is no healing but yours." Meanwhile, in the Qur'an we find Christ saying about himself:

"I heal those born blind, and the lepers." (Surah 3:49)

4) Giving Life and Death:

God is the only one who holds life and death in His hand; no one else can give life or death. The Qur'an says:

"And verily, it is We Who give life and Who give death; it is We Who remain inheritors. (after all else passes away)" (Surah 15:23)

"Verily, We shall give life to the dead, and We record that which they leave behind." (Surah 36:12)

"Verily it is We Who give Life and Death; and to Us is the Final Return." (Surah 50:43)

As for Christ, the Qur'an mentions that he said about himself:

"And I bring the dead into life by Allah's leave." (Surah 3:49)

In his book, *Beginning and End*, Ibn Kathir tells a verified story that proves Christ had the authority to give death as well as life. It is told that Christ saw a woman crying over her daughter, who had died long ago. He asked her, "What makes you cry, woman?" She said, "My daughter died and I have no more children." Christ asked her, "Would you like me to raise her from the dead?" She said, "Yes, O Spirit of God!" So, Christ stood by the grave and called the girl three times. On the third time, the little girl came out and talked with her mother. Then the girl asked Christ to let her return. He told her, "Go back!" The grave closed and she was dead. (*Beginning and End* by Ibn Kathir, part two, page 84)

5) Giving Sustenance:

The Qur'an says:

"For Allah is He Who gives (all) sustenance, Lord of Power, Steadfast (for ever)." (Surah 51:58)

It is clearly stated that God is the only one who can give sustenance. God rebuked anyone who claimed the ability to give sustenance to people. As for Christ, Ibn Kathir mentioned that he had a special ability to give sustenance to whomever he wished. The best example was feeding the five thousand people with little bread and a couple of fish.

6) Matchlessness:

The Qur'an says about God:

"There is nothing whatever like unto Him, and He is the One that hears and sees." (Surah 42:11)

As for Christ, it goes without saying that He is matchless. He was born from a virgin without a man. He was the only one described as 'God's Word and a Spirit from Him.' He was the only one over whom Satan did not have any authority. He was the only one who had divine characteristics.

7) Commanding Authority:

The Qur'an mentions this attribute of God:

"For anything which We have willed, We but say 'Be', and it is." (Surah 16:40)

"When He decreeth a matter, He saith to it: 'Be,' and it is." (Surah 2:117)

This is a unique attribute of God, being able to call something into existence. According to Ibn Kathir, Christ manifested this attribute when he changed the water into wine (Beginning and End by Ibn Kathir, part one, page 85).

8) His Throne Over the Waters:

The Qur'an says about God's throne:

"And His throne was over the waters that He might try you, which of you is best in conduct." (Surah 11:7)

Kortobi and El-Hadathi said that this verse also applied to Christ, whose throne was made by God on the water in order to test people's faith. Christ walked on the Sea of Tiberias towards

His disciples in order to test their faith. He later said to them, "You of little faith." (Matt. 8: 26)

9) Judge and Ruler:

The Qur'an says about God:

"The Command rests with none but Allah: He declares the Truth, and He is the best of judges." (Surah 6:57)

"Hold yourselves in patience until Allah doth decide between us: for He is the best to decide." (Surah 7:87)

El-Bokhary explained that he heard from Ibn Abbas, who had heard the Prophet Mohammed saying about Christ, "The Last Day will not come until the son of Mary comes back as a fair judge to administer justice and wipe out injustice."

10) A Grasp Over All Visions:

The Qur'an says about God:

"No vision can grasp Him, but His grasp is over all vision; He is subtle well-aware." (Surah 6:103)

This is another attribute of God that Christ manifested. Ibn Kathir and Kortobi told a story that Christ was one day on a mountain and the Romans wanted to arrest Him. He went right through them and they could not see him, but He saw them all. (*Sects and Denominations* by Sheheristani, page 27)

11) Most Gracious and Most Merciful:

The Qur'an says:

"And your God is one God: there is no god but He, Most Gracious, Most Merciful." (Surah 2:163)

"Not one of the beings in the heavens and the earth but must come to the Most Gracious as a servant." (Surah 19:93)

In the books *Sects and Denominations* and *Proofs of Prophethood*, Sheheristani and Azraki mentioned that Christ was after the image of God. He was compassionate. He raised the daughter of Jairus from the dead and healed many sick people. He created eyes to the born blind by putting mud on the man's eyes because that's how God created in the beginning.

12) Speaks in Parables:

The Qur'an states that only God can speak in Parables:

"Allah doth set forth Parables for men: and Allah doth know all things." (Surah 24:35)

"So Allah sets forth Parables for men, in order that they

may receive admonition." (Surah 14:25)

In 'El-Kashaf,' Ibn Kathir, Kortobi and Zamakhshary say that God used parables to bring people closer to Him, and so did Christ. The New Testament is full of parables that no other prophet told.

13) Sends Messengers and Gives Them Power:

The Qur'an says:

"Set forth to them, by way of a parable, the (story of) the Companions of the City. Behold, there came messengers to it. When We (first) sent to them two messengers, they rejected them, but We strengthened them with a third." (Surah 36:13)

Ibn Kathir and all interpreters agreed that the mentioned city was Antioch, and the men were messengers of Christ. They had authority from Christ. What other man has such authority?

14) To Be Worshipped:

The Qur'an says:

"The Jews call Uzair a son of Allah, and the Christians call Christ the Son of Allah. That is a saying from their mouth; (in this) they but imitate what the Unbelievers of old used to say... they take their priests and anchorites to be their lords beside Allah, and

mountain and the Romans wanted to arrest Him. He went right
through them and they could not see him, but He saw them all.
(Sects and Denominations by Sheheristani, page 27)

11) Most Gracious and Most Merciful:

The Qur'an says:

"And your God is one God: there is no god but He, Most
Gracious, Most Merciful." (Surah 2:163)

"Not one of the beings in the heavens and the earth but
must come to the Most Gracious as a servant." (Surah
19:93)

In the books Sects and Denominations and Proofs of Prophethood, Sheheristani and Azraki mentioned that Christ was after
the image of God. He was compassionate. He raised the daughter
of Jairus from the dead and healed many sick people. He created
eyes to the born blind by putting mud on the man's eyes because
that's how God created in the beginning.

12) Speaks in Parables:

The Qur'an states that only God can speak in Parables:

"Allah doth set forth Parables for men: and Allah doth
know all things." (Surah 24:35)

"So Allah sets forth Parables for men, in order that they may receive admonition." (Surah 14:25)

In 'El-Kashaf,' Ibn Kathir, Kortobi and Zamakhshary say that God used parables to bring people closer to Him, and so did Christ. The New Testament is full of parables that no other prophet told.

13) Sends Messengers and Gives Them Power:

The Qur'an says:

"Set forth to them, by way of a parable, the (story of) the Companions of the City. Behold, there came messengers to it. When We (first) sent to them two messengers, they rejected them, but We strengthened them with a third." (Surah 36:13)

Ibn Kathir and all interpreters agreed that the mentioned city was Antioch, and the men were messengers of Christ. They had authority from Christ. What other man has such authority?

14) To Be Worshipped:

The Qur'an says:

"The Jews call Uzair a son of Allah, and the Christians call Christ the Son of Allah. That is a saying from their mouth; (in this) they but imitate what the Unbelievers of old used to say... they take their priests and anchorites to be their lords beside Allah, and Christ the son of Mary." (Surah 9:30)

Ibn Kotaiba sees this as a problematic verse, because it puts worshipping God and Christ as a commandment. So, Ibn Kotaiba thought in order to avoid this problem the phrase 'Christ the son of Mary' should be syntactically interpreted as a 'second object' to the verb 'take' and not an 'annexment' to the word 'Allah.' This way the verse would not support the Christian view of Christ's deity.

15) Comes in Clouds:

The Qur'an says:

"Will they wait until Allah comes to them in canopies of clouds?" (Surah 2:210)

Ibn El-Fadl El-Hadathi said that this verse referred to Christ who would come back on the Last Day on clouds. He also interpreted the following verse as referring to Christ, too:

"And thy Lord cometh, and His angels, rank upon rank." (Surah 89:22)

As a matter of fact, I found out more than I was looking for. I wrote my findings in a separate booklet titled, 'The Inevitability of Christ's Deity.' I originally called it 'Christ's Divinity,' but after I finished my research I had to change the title to 'The Inevitability of Christ's Deity.' I concluded the booklet with the following sentence, "Even if Christians did not claim Christ was God, He had to be God."

As for the second part, namely Christ's death as a sacrifice for the sinners, Muslim always rejected this idea because the Qur'an said:

"No bearer of burdens can bear the burden of another." (Surah 17:15)

How could an innocent die for sinners? Well, we had another dilemma: did Christ really die? I was very confident – I don't know why – that I would not find anything to prove the death of Christ. I had searched and did not find any evidence that would appease my conscience and strengthen my faith in Islam. Therefore, I was so anxious to counter the evidence of Christ's Deity by proving that He did not die, and could not have died for sinners.

I was trying to refute the idea of 'Sacrificial Death' when I came across the following verse in the Qur'an:

"And remember Moses said to his people: 'O my people! Ye have indeed wronged yourselves by your worship of the calf: So turn (in repentance) to your Maker, and slay yourselves (the wrong-doers); that will be better for you in the sight of your Maker." (Surah 2:54)

I read Ibn Kathir's interpretation of this verse. He said that the Israelites wanted to repent of their sin of worshipping the calf, but God did not accept their repentance. When Moses mediated, God told him to tell the Israelites that the only way to get forgiveness was that each man should kill everybody he met. It is said that they put on blindfolds so they would not have mercy on their families, but would have the courage to obey God's order. Ibn Kathir said that at least seventy thousand were killed that day, and blood ran like a stream. When God saw it was enough, He told Moses to tell the Israelites to stop. God accepted their repentance through the blood of those who died. If someone did not worship the calf and died as atonement for those who did, why would we reject the idea that the sinless Christ died for sinners, and that He was still alive?

I felt God was encircling me with evidences and I had no way to reject Christ's call for me to follow Him. I even found many references to the death of Christ. I read Ibn Kathir's interpretation of Surah 4:157 and other verses from Surah 3 that spoke of the death of Christ. Actually, people differed not on the death of Christ, but on how long it was. The stories varied between three hours, one day and two days. This proves the actual death of Christ.

I grew more angry and frustrated because I wanted to find anything to refute Christian beliefs. I was proud of my religion and myself, and I hated Christians. Meanwhile, I had no choice but to adjust to the new situation, but how?

I never stopped reading the Bible. It became a friend of mine. The more I read, the more I tasted its sweetness. One time while reading I was stunned by the following verses:

"And when you pray, do not be like the hypocrites, for they love to pray standing in the synagogues and on the street corners to be seen by men. I tell you the truth; they have received their reward in full. But when you pray, go into your room, close the door and pray to your Father, who is unseen. Then your Father, who sees what is done in secret, will reward you." (Mt. 6:5-6)

I was amazed how the Bible recorded, two thousand years ago, these things that happened in the present time. I remembered the time when I used to put something hard under my forehead when I knelt down during prayers in order to brag about my 'prayer mark.' I used to boast about my fasting and worship. I even wore certain outfits to show that I was religious.

I searched the issue of Christ's death and crucifixion, and whether Christ actually died. I studied all the Christian books and references that dealt with the 'Sacrificial Death of Christ.' Finally, my mind was almost convinced of Christ's divinity and crucifixion. Some people might think that I was pleased with my findings. On the contrary, I was so upset, frustrated and tense. I wished God had killed me before I found out that I had lived all my life with false beliefs. It was so hard on me to find out that those repulsive, filthy Christians were right and I was wrong.

I could not sleep a wink. I roamed the streets talking to myself. Thoughts tore me apart; doubts shook my being whenever I started to pray. I did not know what to do. I asked the brothers to visit me less often. I invented an excuse that I was under police surveillance. Gradually I grew apart from the whole group. I would feel sleepy whenever I recited the Qur'an everyday as usual. On the other hand, I could not read enough of the Bible. I was very much attached to that Book. One day, the Emir visited me and found out that I had not made any substantial progress in my research. He said to me, "It's the will of Allah! Give us the Bible and we'll find somebody else to do the job instead of you. It seems you're not cut out for such a task."

I was supposed to be happy because that was what I wanted, but things were different. I asked him to give me one more month because I had managed to put my finger on some essential clues. The truth was I did not want to lose my permission to read the Bible, and the Book itself. The Emir agreed. I did not know why I did so. I could have agreed to give the Bible back and save myself all the strain and the unknown future that I was heading for. Every time I got ready to pray I heard an inner voice asking me, "How could you pray to a god you are not sure exists?" It made me cry.

One time, I resisted that inner voice and started reading the Qur'an. I came across a verse that captured my attention:

"And dispute ye not with the People of the Book, except in the best way, unless it be with those of them who do wrong but say, 'We believe in the Revelation which has come down to us and in that which came down to you; our God and your God is One; and it is to Him we submit (in Islam)." (Surah 29:46)

I wanted to study this verse more in depth, so I referred to the commentaries written by Ibn Kathir, Kortobi and Zamakhshary. First thing I found out was that they all agreed that this verse was abrogated by the famous verse of the 'Sword' in Surah 9. Abrogation was only part of the problem. I noticed that the verse stated that our God and the People of the Book's God were one and the same. I could not go on; my mind stopped! God had abrogated all previous kindliness towards non-Muslims and replaced it with killing, torture and hurting. He even made us, Muslims, His instrument of torture:

"Fight them, and Allah will punish them by your hands, and disgrace them." (Surah 9:14)

In the Qur'an there are more than 27 verses speaking about the fact that Muslims are obliged to fight non-Muslims. Meanwhile, the God of Christians says:

"But I tell you who hear me: Love your enemies, do good to those who hate you, bless those who curse you, pray for those who mistreat you." (Luke. 6:27-28)

"But I tell you, do not resist an evil person. If someone strikes you on the right cheek, turn to him the other also. And if someone wants to sue you and take your tunic, let him have your cloak as well. If someone forces you to go one mile, go with him two miles." (Mt. 5:39-41)

I started comparing these verses to what the Qur'an says:

"If then anyone transgresses the prohibition against you, transgress ye likewise against him." (Surah 2:194)

"Against them make ready your strength to the utmost of your power, including steeds of war, to strike terror into (the hearts of) the enemies of Allah and your enemies." (Surah 8:59)

"Mohammed is the Messenger of Allah; and those who are with him are strong against Unbelievers, (but) compassionate amongst each other." (Surah 48:29)

It is impossible that White and Black would be one; or Good and Evil would be one; or Day and Night would be one! One has to be distinctly unique. So, there should be only one God. I was sure to find that God, because I loved Him. No one would prevent me from believing in the One True God, even if He were the God of Jews!

In my mind, I talked to God, "Oh, God, I need your help. Do not forsake me for I'm now confused. I don't know where you are. If I was misled, it was not on purpose. You know how much I love you, and how much I suffered for your sake. Oh, God, if you're punishing me for some sin I committed, I ask for your forgiveness. You are the only God and I am your servant, who obeys your commandments. I confess my sins and repent. Please don't be so harsh in your punishment."

Certain thoughts made me shiver out of awe and fear. I thought that the Qur'an and the Bible could not both be the Word of God. One had to annul the other. I panicked when this thought crossed my mind. Whenever I heard a strange sound I thought that God would destroy the house and make it fall on my head because of my attitude towards the Qur'an. My life became unbearable! It was even harder than the time I was imprisoned and tortured.

Soon, this feeling subsided and I decided to study the Qur'an afresh in order to review every possible aspect and to evaluate the verse objectively:

"Had it been from other than Allah, they would surely have found therein much discrepancy." (Surah 4:82)

As a matter of fact, I was not objective. I wished to find something in the Qur'an to lead me to believe that it was not from God. I had deep bitterness towards Christians. I would have accepted anything but to become a Christian. The word 'Christian' provoked me, and aroused in me a strong desire of aggression and revenge towards anything related to Christians. I did not know why I felt this way; perhaps it was due to my upbringing in a strict family that loved Islam and hated Christianity, assuming the latter was infidelity. Our parents used to warn us not to play with Christian kids because they were traitors, and not to eat their food because they could poison us. We were raised to think that Christians had no god, no faith and no trust.

I started to study the Qur'an in depth and I found out amazing things that I had never noticed before. I compiled my research and titled it, *"Is the Qur'an the Word of God?"* It took me about six months to finish it.

One day, the Emir paid me an unexpected visit. I was in the restroom when he came. My mother let him into my room because he was well known to my family, since we had been in prison together. The Emir saw papers scattered around the room and thought that I finished a good part of my assignment. I heard him saying, "Allah bless you! You're the man! I was right; you're the only one who could do it!" I thought in my mind, "You don't know what's on these papers!"

A moment later, I came out to meet him. His face was red and he seemed flabbergasted. He pulled me by the collar and screamed in my face, "What is this? Did you write that? It could not be you. Who deceived you? Who tricked you? Who tempted you to sell out your religion?"

I said to him, "If there was deception, it would be yours; if there was temptation it would be from you; if I committed a sin, it would be on your head! You're the one who pushed me to all this. I wanted to be relieved of this research and you refused. You knew how much I hated Christianity and Christians, but you insisted that I read their books. I swear to you I wish everything I found out they were untrue. You and I shared the most difficult time of our lives, didn't we?" He said, "Yes." I said, "Did you notice anything unusual?" He said, "No." I said, "Excuse me, it's out of my hand. It's not just a matter of information; it's my heart, over which I have no power. I wish you would read what I read and learned what I learned!"

He went berserk and wanted to tear all my the papers (Deity of Christ, the Qur'an is not the Word of God, etc.) We had a major argument that brought my mother to the room. Before leaving my house, the Emir said to me, "Now we know what's wrong with you, but I have a demand if you want to stay alive." "What is it?" I asked. "Don't ever tell your group about this poison you're writing. I will tell them that you apostatized, but I won't give them any reasons. If you tell them anything else you know what will happen to you," he replied.

I said to him, "What you don't seem to realize is that times have changed. You know that I don't get threatened because you're not able to carry out your threats. For your information, I was faithful to my brothers when I asked them not to visit me. I could not continue teaching them something I wasn't sure was true. I pushed them away because I cared for them. I promise you, I love God, and I pray that He will bring me back if I have gone astray."

I broke in tears as I remembered our beautiful memories, our life together in prison and how we faced hardships together. To be honest, it was too much for me to take. But if this is the will of God, then good bye to all good memories away from Him and welcome to all thorns on His side.

The group started to cut all ties with me. Members avoided me, and did not even greet me on the street. I knew immediately that I had been pronounced an infidel. They took back the money they give me from the group's 'House of Treasury' for my personal expenses. They thought that would break me and force me back to the group. They never understood me.

The Emir and I, together with some other people, had an investment company. We used the large amounts of money that we brought from abroad to buy and sell clothes. I was the official manager who signed checks. I was legally responsible for the business. When I refused to repent, they did not pay their share and took me to court. They expected me to apologize and repent for my infidelity. At the courthouse, the Emir came to me and whispered, "We could drop the charges if you came to your senses and repented to Allah, and told us who misled you." I didn't answer.

The court sentenced me to pay the money back in the form of monthly installments of 160 Egyptian Pounds. It was a blow to them because they wanted to see me go to jail. I thanked God that the trial went well, but I spoke to God in a bitter, angry way: "Oh, God, why do you do this to me? Why do I have to suffer? Since I was a child I have suffered and struggled. I have no more friends because they don't believe in you. I lost the love of my family because they did not accept you. I lost my studies because they stood between you and me. Now, I don't know what pain you have in store for me. Please, have mercy on me. I'm weak and powerless. Don't leave me for the waves to throw me around in this rough sea. I don't know where to go. Tell me where you are. Are you the God of Christians? The God of Moses? The God of Mohammed? If you were the God of Mohammed, why would you leave me to suffer and doubt you? Please, God, don't leave me alone. I promise to follow you wherever you are. I fear nobody but you, and you know that very well."

Suddenly my train of thoughts was interrupted by my mother's voice asking me to take my food. I didn't eat with my mother because I believed a Muslim should not eat with an infidel – and according to the group, my mother was one.

I then came to a very critical question: if the Qur'an was not from God, then who is Mohammed? He had to be a false prophet. But how do I prove that? I suddenly panicked and thought, "It couldn't be! Mohammed is a false prophet? What about his miracles and his empire, and all the multitudes who followed him?

I felt like I was about to face God's wrath and torture. When I cooled down I felt a strange courage and a strong will to focus my research on who Mohammed was, and whether he was a prophet or not. I found out that Mohammed's claim to prophethood was based on two aspects: he was illiterate, but he received the Qur'an; and he was infallible – before he became a prophet, he never committed a sin.

ILLITERACY

I was completely out of my mind to find a proof that Mohammad could read and write. All that I knew was that it was impossible that Mohammad could read and write. This issue motivated me to read once again the Prophet's biographies. In fact, to my great astonishment I found many issues I hadn't noticed before. I discovered that Mohammad used to go to the same place where El-Nadr Ibn El-Hareth, Waraka Ibn Nofal and Ibn Sa'eda, the well-known priest, used to go. I also found out that Mohammad used to conduct business with the big fortunes of the rich lady Khadija and that he made many contracts and agreements with the merchants of Yemen and Greater Syria.

It was said that Mohammad carried with him a stamp he used instead of a signature, which meant that he was illiterate. But carrying that stamp did not mean that he was illiterate since it was commonplace among merchants of that time to write the contract between the merchant and the customer, and then stamp it for authorization like the Seal of the Republic nowadays.

I discovered that, after the peace treaty of Al-Hudaibiya, Mohammad wrote the reconciliation treaty with his own hands, that he was under the custody of his uncle Abu Taleb, and that he was older than Ali. Ali could read and write and it was unimaginable that Mohammad would not learn even the minimum basic level of reading and writing.

I found out that Mohammad used to sit with Yassar Al-Nusrani (the Christian) and to take from him the texts of the Bible and read them. I realized when the angel Gabriel came to Mohammad and asked him to read that it was not logical on Gabriel's part to ask Mohammad to read, knowing that he was illiterate! If you add all the above-mentioned issues to what I discovered regarding the authenticity of the prophethood of Mohammad, you will come to the realization that Mohammad was neither a prophet nor a righteous man. You can find all the details of this issue in a book I prepared titled, Mohammad in the Torah and the Bible.

INERRANCY

s for Mohammad's inerrancy, there are many biographies such as "Al-Seera Al-Halabiya," "Al-Tabakaat Al-Kubra" and " Seerat Ibn Hisham" even the commentaries that dealt with Surah 16:

"And from the fruit of the date-palm and the vine, Ye get out strong drink." (Surah 16:67)

There are many authentic Hadiths stating clearly that Mohammad used to drink wine and recommended that his friends put some water into wine if it was highly concentrated. He used to eat from the animal sacrifices offered by Kuraish at El-Ka'ba for idols. He allowed the forbidden and forbade the allowed by God.

He was making eyes at the women of his friends, and he never hesitated to take any one of them if she pleased him. At the Day of Kheibar, Safiyya, daughter of Yehiah Ibn Akhtab, came under the lot of Abdallah Ibn Umar. But Mohammad took her from him and married her. He also took Zainab daughter of Gahsh, the wife of Zaid (his adopted son), to be one of his wives.

All those events demolished any hallowed picture of Mohammad and blew up the sacred status I used to ascribe to the Prophet Mohammad. To be honest with you, I was in pain whenever I discovered any thing like this.

With all that I found out about Mohammad, honestly speaking, I was still hoping to find any virtues in Islam to clutch at in order to remain a Muslim. It was hard for me to leave the religion of my childhood. Whenever I toyed with the idea of leaving Islam, strange feelings of fear, confusion and turmoil would assail my mind. Whenever I read any magnificent and meaningful text in the Bible, my hatred, hostility and cruelty would increase against Christians. I had a Christian colleague. Whenever I found something great in the Bible, my anger was kindled and I went and destroyed his belongings to let out my bottled-up rage. I paid money to others to conspire against him and send false complaints against him to the high authorities. One day, I set all his clothes on fire and he had to go back home in his work uniform.

I used to stand before one of the shops owned by a Christian man, preventing people from buying from him and accusing him of being a cheater. I would say to people on the street, "Do not buy from Christians; they are evasive swindlers. They want to destroy Islam. The Qur'an said, 'They have no faith.'" That old Christian man used to say to me: "Oh my son, what have I done to you? Have mercy; I have to earn money to raise my children."

Other times, I would warn my friends against shaking hands with Christians, observing the Hadith, "Do not shake hands with the People of the Book; do not greet them and make their way narrow." I often would shout, "They are malicious, showing a fake love but they are arch enemies to Allah and true believers. Don't be deceived by their counterfeit humiliation. God said: 'They were covered with humiliation and misery.'"

On one of those hectic days, teeming with all such deeds against Christians, I felt a hunch in my heart of hearts. There was an inner voice telling me, "Be honest with yourself. Do you think all such acts could remove all that you have learned from their Books? You said that you would follow God wherever that would lead you; so why, whenever God would reveal to you some light of inspiration, do you try to put it out? Be honest with yourself in order to have a clear conscience. Check you inner motives. Do you really want God? If otherwise, what do you really want? It is all up to you. It is all in your hands and nobody will force you into anything."

I went back home, weighed down with lots of burdens. I tried to pray, but I couldn't. I began to read the Bible and I came across the prayer of Christ in the Gospel of Matthew. When I read that prayer, I suddenly felt a strange sense of peace, tranquility and calmness covering me. It was as if one had poured water to cleanse my memory from something. I said in my heart of hearts,

"Oh my Lord, can you give me that kind of peace, patience, love and endurance that the Christians used to have if I pray exactly as it is written in the Bible?"

I was beside myself with joy as if I heard the answer, "Yes." My face lit up with pleasure and I made up my mind to pray the Lord's Prayer regularly. I would get up early at dawn, the same time of ritual prayers, but would pray the Lord's Prayer this time. I would also complete my ablution and spread the prayer carpet on the ground as I used to do in the past. Then I would stand on it and say:

"Our Father who art in Heaven,

Hallowed be Your name,

Your kingdom come.

Your will be done

On earth as it is in heaven.

Give us this day our daily bread.

And forgive our debts

As we forgive our debtors.

And do not lead us into temptation.

But deliver us from the evil one."

Finally, I would conclude by saying: "Peace be upon you and the Mercy of God, Peace be upon you and the Mercy of God." (the Islamic conclusion of prayers.)

I continued like that for quite a long time, but I did not notice any change in my character. I was still aggressive with my family and with Christians. So, I decided to do away with all religions. Neither Islam nor Christianity worked. Perhaps after converting to Christianity, I would read a book, only to find some other, better religion after a while, spending all the rest of my life jumping from one religion to another. The best thing to do in such case, I thought, was to lead a normal life like others, like ordinary people. Why should I overload my mind with all that religion stuff? Let me enjoy a carefree life and when I die, let God do whatever He wants with me!

But that was not a real solution. All of a sudden, an idea came to my mind. I said to myself that the reason for all my problems and confusion was that Book, the Torah and the Bible, so let me tear it into pieces and be done with it forever. I was about to do so, but I felt a shiver in my body and an inner voice whispering in my mind, "Leave it. You may need it some time. Why do you want to get rid of that particular book? The Qur'an has caused you far much more trouble. Why didn't you want to tear it into pieces?"

Whenever I would ride in a car, I would pray that the car would be in an accident and every one in it would be rescued except for me. I also wished, from the bottom of my heart that the house would tumble upon my head that I alone would die. "Oh Lord," I said, "If you do not wish to give me guidance, it is better that you would finish my life and let me get out of my dilemma."

I was in the middle of that turmoil of conflicting thoughts. It was four o'clock in the afternoon of one of the summer days of July. I was sitting by myself, reminiscing, thinking about my long associations with Islam, Islamic Groups and terrorism, and finally, with the New Testament and the Torah. I prayed: "Oh God, you know that, in all these events, I was searching for you. Is it fair to leave me in such a condition? Where is your justice and love? Even if you want to punish me for a crime I committed, I think, by now, I have already paid for all my crimes. What crime requires such a severe punishment? Please God; do not leave me alone in such a struggle."

Suddenly, I saw the door of my room open. I thought it was my mother bringing me something to eat. And behold, there was a hulk of a man with long hair and heavy beard and a pillar of white radiating light beside him. It was like light coming from a great number of florescent lamps put together. I could not look at his face or fix my eyes upon him. I heard him calling me, "Stand up; the Christ wants you." In no time, I jumped out of my room. I was flabbergasted and I called my father, mother and brothers to come and see the Christ (our Master Isa) since it was written in Al-Bukhari Book that he who would see a prophet had seen 'guidance,' since demons did not take the form of prophets. I said to myself that my family might believe if they saw the Christ.

I went back to my room to see nothing. I was shocked from head to toe. I was deeply distressed. How could I prove this to my family? I blamed God for not helping me, "Why didn't you wait in the room so that they would see you and come to believe? They will think of me as one who has lost his mind."

That was exactly what happened. All my family members went into my room only to find nothing unusual. My mother said, "Oh

Lord, why do you allow all this to happen to us. We were glad to have our son back and now you let him go mad!" She started crying bitterly and she hugged me. My brother told me not to worry for he would take me to the best psychiatrist in Egypt. My sisters said, "All this is from what you write during the night. The end of all this is madness. Oh God, please heal him."

After all of them finished their lamentations, I said to them, "Aren't you so and so?" Each said, "Yes." I went to my mother and said to her, "Aren't you my mother?" She said, "Yes." "Aren't you my brother?" He said, "Yes." I went to my sister and said, "Aren't you my sister?" She said, "Yes." I said to them, "If I were insane as you think, how could I know all of you by name? Why don't you believe me? I have seen him as a great light. He spoke to me." But their viewpoint was stronger than my argument. Finally, I started to believe them. I must be really mad. So I went to my bed and stayed there. I must have lost my senses. What I say lacks common sense. I remained in my room and my brothers would come to me to comfort me, but I uttered nothing. I resorted to complete silence.

The following morning, my brother took me to one of the best psychiatrists in the country. We went to his clinic and I waited my turn. Finally, they called me to see the doctor. I sat before him and he asked me, "How can I help you?" I told him, "I don't know. My brother decided to bring me to you." He said, "Your brother said that you have seen our Master the Christ!" I said, "Yes, I have seen him indeed." He said: "Can you describe him to me?" I asked him, "Have you seen him before?" He said, "No." I said, "If you don't know what he looks like, how can you know if I am right or not?" He said, "Your case is a very hard one."

He called for my brother from the waiting room. When he came into the examining room, the doctor told him that I had a severe case of depression and I needed electric treatment quickly. I started with six sessions of electric treatment and gradually it was reduced to two. He asked my brother to bring me to the hospital twice a week. My brother told him that it was hard to do so since we lived in a town far from Cairo and it would take us two and half hours of driving. My brother suggested that the doctor tell us how we could have such a treatment in our town through any other doctor. He agreed and so did I. I told him that I was not afraid of electric treatment, as I had already experienced them when I was tortured in concentration camps. I was sure that medical treatment would be less severe than those electric shocks we used to endure in the torture rooms.

I did not find any reason to refuse the electric treatment. If I were really mad, this would help me gain my sanity back. If not, this pain would be added to other painful experiences I had during my search for God; hopefully, God would take that into consideration and have mercy on me.

Eventually, I completed my treatment sessions and I took all the medications that my doctor prescribed. I expected that I would be healed by then and would forget all the thoughts that used to torment me if they were brought by madness or psychosomatic tension. However, I found myself urged to read more in the Bible. I couldn't sleep unless I read a part of the Bible. I decided to keep all my findings to myself and tell nobody of any experience I might have from that time on. I decided to live as a Christian to see the work of God. If this were the way, surely I would see the fruits of it. I wanted to see God's support of this choice; otherwise I would brush it aside.

As I previously said, I used to pray regularly, in my own way, five times per day: at dawn, noon, dusk, sunset, and evening. I did not read anything in my prayers but the Lord's Prayer. But I was perplexed as to which religious practices I had to perform to make my prayers complete and acceptable in order to gain some merit before God. I had to go to the church to learn how I can worship God. I did not like the idea of going to church. How could I go to the church in such a state? How could I go to church in a state of humility and submission, as I was so antagonistic in the past? "No, I will not go to church. Maybe some other time," I said to myself.

I tried to ask some Christians for help, but who would agree to speak with me after all that I had done to them? All of them refused to meet me. They thought either I wanted to kill them or force them to be converted to Islam. Finally, one of them agreed to meet me in a month. I had to wait for that time. I decided to use that time in reading more about the Christian beliefs and concepts. I wanted to know what they said and whether they had their own Christian books similar to what the Muslims had.

First of all, I decided to shave off my beard just to look normal. I borrowed a shirt and a pair of pants instead of wearing the 'Galabia' (Islamic outfit) that I used to wear all my life. I went to the bookstore where I got my Holy Bible. I did not like any of the books in that bookstore, so I decided to go to another one nearby. I began to look through the shelves, from outside the store, to see what kind of books they carried. I did not dare to enter a 'Christian' bookstore. I couldn't even look at anything Christian; so how could I enter now a Christian place? I was afraid they might ask to see my ID (ID's in Egypt state one's religion) and they might call the police. I would, then, fall into the hands of the Secret State Intelligence, which was like going to the bottomless pit.

After a long time of hesitation, I took heart and entered the bookstore. Some books caught my attention. I did not know what sort of books I wanted to read. Whenever I came across a title that would catch my attention, I would buy the book. I bought the books, *"Evidence That Requests A Decision," "My Faith,"* and *"Atonement of Christ."* As soon as I finished reading one of the books, I burned it.

When I finished all those books, I went back to the bookstore to get some more. I found two books: *"Monotheism and Trinity,"* and *"Biblical Theology."* When I looked at the prices of those two books, I knew that I did not have enough money to buy them. So I put them on the shelves. At that moment, an old man approached me and asked, "Why did you put the books back?" I said, "I don't want them." "If you don't want them, why have you taken them in the first place?" he said. I snapped back with, "That's none of your business. What is this – a interrogation?" He put his hand on my shoulder and his face showed a trace of a gentle smile. He said: "My son, take the books and I will pay for them. I will give you my address. If you like them, you can pay me back. If not, you can get rid of them or burn them – you have nothing to lose." I asked him how he knew that I didn't have the money to buy the books. He told me that the Holy Spirit told him. I said in my heart of hearts, "What is this Holy Spirit?" I thought a lot about that question.

I went with him to his house. We sat together for a few minutes. I was afraid he might ask to see my ID. In that case, he would know the truth. But all things went smoothly, thank God. The man didn't even ask my name.

I kept on reading those books and others diligently, either at home or I would rent a hotel room to enjoy all the time reading on my own without any disturbance. I did not want to waste a minute even to eat. I wanted to devour all the Words of Christ that would take me at least one step further to the new road of my new life.

I used to frequent a coffee shop where many of the customers were Christians. There I would read all the Christian books I bought. I loved the teachings of the Bible. To be more accurate, my desire was to be that type of person portrayed in the Bible. If I would live accordingly, I would turn into an angel walking on earth.

I was preoccupied with questions: "If I receive you and walk according to your Bible, Lord, is it possible for you to make me better? Can I have some friends even if they don't believe as I do? Can I love my mother, father, brothers and sisters even if they don't accept my new beliefs? Can I love my friends even if they don't share my faith or believe what I say? Can you do this for me, Lord? Can I love my country and feel the same loyalty as other people?"

The first step the Islamic group took to disciple any newcomer was to uproot any other loyalty, whether to the homeland, family or anything else. One should have no other loyalty but to Allah, and no other devotion but to the Emir. That's why I didn't believe I could change or love. My last vision of light and that person who said to me, "Stand up, the Christ wants you" was a real source of much perplexity. I knew that any vision of one of the prophets was a divine guidance, but what kind of divine guidance? Was it guidance toward the Christian or the Muslim faith?

My mind was tossed by all these thoughts that I rapidly walked the streets as if somebody was chasing me. This was a terrible time, I didn't know where to go. At last, I made up my mind to go to a church. I wanted to be the man God wanted me to be. I heard an inner voice saying, "Now you have heard the voice and you have to follow it. You have lived in Islam all your life, but you haven't lived yet in Christianity to know what it is like. You haven't lived the Christian faith to know which is better or nearer to God, Christianity or Islam."

I went to many churches. It was not easy to do so. I had to struggle against the Devil whenever I decided to enter a church. The Devil would whisper in my ears, "Have you reached that miserable status as to go to a church? Shame on you! How much difference it is between going to the church now in humiliation and when you went there to exalt the Word of Allah. Have your forgotten what you did to the church in the past? If you forgot, I can remind you. You used to say: 'Truth has (now) arrived, and Falsehood perished; for falsehood is (by its nature) bound to perish.' Where is that truth for which you have exposed your life to death? You have nowhere to go but to the church – the den of infidelity, polytheism and blasphemy. Are you going to believe in more than one God after all that long journey of loyalty and faithfulness to the only God? Wake up; repent to God and ask His forgiveness and repeat the two Shehadas (Testimonies): 'I witness that there is no God but Allah and that Mohammad is His Messenger.' Get up and wash yourself of all these evil thoughts and take refuge in Allah against the abominable Devil."

After that, I found myself unconsciously going to church. It was still difficult and I would feel as if somebody was pulling me back to prevent me from going. I even shouted, "I will go to church. I will go to church; come what may. I will go there, no matter what." It was enough that I had no more friends and family members. I hadn't known mercy all my life. I had killed and robbed and now I stood without relatives, friends, companions or any of God's creation. Could God be happy with me in such condition? Does God approve of killing, hatred, hostility and vandalism towards all who refused to accept what we say?

I said: "Oh God, have mercy on me. I am a miserable and lonely person. I want to lead a normal life, loving my country, family, and friends. But how can I do this?"

So I decided to go to church even if it would have cost me my life. I rushed towards the church. I didn't expect the attitude of the priest. He refused to listen to me, which added fuel to fire and aggravated the devilish attacks against me. When I went out of the church that day, I felt some sort of inner relief within me despite having failed to convince the pastor to listen to me. It actually encouraged me to try again. Unfortunately, I failed in all my attempts to sit with any pastor and to learn what I could do to deserve the salvation of Christ. The text says, "Whoever believes and is baptized will be saved." I was preoccupied with the questions, "How can I believe? What can I do? How can I pray, fast, go to pilgrimage, or pay alms?"

The last time I left church, I was so burdened and heavily laden, as they say, "covered with burning shame." Satan whispered in my ears, "They have rejected you. It serves you right. You deserve more than that and God will show you harder lessons." But the demonic harassment did not last long. I heard a quiet and gentle voice from within saying, "Hey you, you do not worship people; don't be upset by their behavior towards you. Since you worship God, only He will not let you down. He will never disappoint you or let you go astray. Just be patient, if you are really searching for Him then hold firm to Him. The days of your suffering will not be long. God will never reject all those who seek Him. Haven't you read, "Come to me, all you who are weary and burdened, and I will give you rest"? (Matt. 11:28) I said to him, "I have read it Lord, if not now, at least I have read it several times written on the wall of a church I passed by everyday on my way to medical school." I knew that verse by heart and I knew the church building that had seen the verse on it. It was the very building where I used to close my eyes trying not to see it.

The voice said, "Give your life to God and He will bring it to pass." I said, "Oh God, I give you my life. Please save me from my circumstances. Teach me your ways. I am at a loss. I am perplexed. This happens to me quite often, Lord." Whenever I would go through a hard turn, I would go back to the Bible to find a wonderful sense of peace and inner calmness.

I tried to get in touch with some of the Christians who used to work with me, but they were not happy to see me and, in fact, were afraid of me. They remembered how I would trap and hurt them. Other Christians refused to talk with me, believing that my aim was to convert them to Islam. But if God wants something, nobody can stand against Him. Once, I went with an engineer friend of mine to visit one of his friends. On our way back, he sarcastically asked me to visit a Christian friend of his. He knew how much I hated Christians. He thought by this sarcasm he would make fun of me, not expecting me to agree so quickly to go. He asked me, again, "Are you sure you want to visit that person? You know he is a Christian?" I replied, "Yes, I know, and want to go with you and visit him." He asked me not to mistreat that man. I promised him to behave.

We went to that Christian friend who knew me well. I used to confront him on the street and incite other Muslims against him, attempting to force him to be a Muslim. As soon as he saw me standing at his door, he was speechless. He closed the door immediately and went back inside. My friend kept on knocking on his door. Finally, he opened the door and started criticizing my friend. He said, "How can you bring that man to my house? Have you forgotten what he did to me? Have mercy on me. I am a man of peace and I have enough problems."

After some pointed words, he allowed us in. In his apartment, a big Bible caught my attention. It was situated on a small table in the middle of the room. I took the Bible and turned some pages. I asked him, "Is this your Holy Book?" He mumbled and stumbled with a shaky voice, "Yes, it is, and the Qur'an also is a Holy Book. All Books are from God. All are 'OK,' the Qur'an and the Bible, Mohammad and the Christ. All are good." It was crystal clear he was terrified. He was afraid of me that whenever I tried to approach him, he would move back. We ended up making circles around each other, crossing the living room, back and forth, as if we were playing hide and seek. Finally, he was in a corner and I stood right in front of him so he could not go anywhere. I said to him, "Why are you doing this? I just want to talk to you."

Knowing that my friend had gone into another room to get some rest, I took the chance and tried to start a conversation with my host. I was eager to achieve my goal of learning the Christian's road to God; but he did not cooperate. I asked him if I could visit him some other time. He agreed, as long as we were not alone. He wanted to have some friends present. I told him that it was fine with me. He wrote down his address and at the time we agreed I visited him only to find half a dozen of his friends at his apartment.

He was so afraid of me. I talked with him for a while. I did not deny that I was talking like a defeated military commander making peaceful negotiations with the victorious commander. I put my head down. I was so ashamed that I looked down all the time. I remembered what I used to be. Now here I was, begging a Christian for some words that would lead me to what I used to fight against. But it was the peace of God and the desire for salvation that pushed me to sacrifice all in order to gain the privilege of entering the Kingdom of God for which I had been unceasingly searching. I had left no stone unturned, searching every nook and cranny to reach my cherished and long awaited goal. Now I was only a stone's throw from the goal. I discovered that my goal could be found nowhere but between the pages of that Book that belonged to my Christian friend.

I was ready to leave no stone unturned to get to know the way of the Lord. My newfound Christian friend had little knowledge of the Bible, so he was not able to give me any more information. He had family problems and I heard from some friends that he was considering converting to Islam in order to be able to marry another wife. I was so irritated by such a solution; I was full of contempt towards him. I felt that he was certainly unable to provide me with what I needed.

After a while, my relationship with him grew stronger, and I had the chance to visit with him more than once. He provided me a quiet place where I could read freely. He did not try to force me to accept any kind of particular thought. I had one specific approach and that was to know the Lord Jesus Christ apart from all factions and denominations, avoiding what I had suffered from in Islam.

Things did not go the way they should have. Our friendship did not last long, but I was introduced to another Christian who was well versed in the knowledge of the Bible. However, we were at odds with each other, to say the least. In the past, whenever he would ask me to do something for him in my work, I would give him wrong information. I would also instigate people against him. I would even reward them if they caused him harm. I didn't expect him to be willing to meet me. Surprisingly, he agreed to meet me in one month but he asked me to confirm our appointment by calling him one week before we were to meet.

I felt that the circle was getting smaller around me. There were no pastors of churches to listen to me, no individuals willing to meet with me. My position was in doubt in the eyes of all Christians. It was difficult for them just to mention my name. If anyone who wanted to threaten others, it was enough to tell them, "I will tell Mr. So and so." I was like a scarecrow scaring birds from the field. Three weeks later, I had to contact that person to confirm our appointment. Since I didn't have a phone in my house I went out to use a public phone.

Whenever I would go out, I used to take all my papers and memos to make sure they would not fall into the wrong hands. It would be very dangerous if anyone saw these notes since I had many pages of research about the Deity of Christ, the fallibility of the Qur'an, Mohammed's prophethood and whether he was really a prophet, etc. I used to carry all those papers, along with the Bible, in a plastic bag whenever I went out.

When I went out to call that person, I was shocked to find that the whole plastic bag with all the papers had just vanished into thin air. Everything was gone – my wallet, my ID, the Bible and all the research. Amazingly, I had a strange kind of peace, calmness and tranquility that I developed first in my dealings with the security officers and secret police. The sole preoccupation of my mind at that time centered on two things:

First, the one who stole my bag might read all my papers and send them to the State Security Investigations Department. I would then be an easy prey in their hands as my ID card was included with the papers, making it so easy to identify me. I could be executed for attacking the Qur'an; capital punishment is the only possible sentence in such a case. However, this subject did not bother me so much since I was quite certain that when my time would come to meet my Creator, I could not delay even for a split second. Every soul, for sure, would taste death.

Second, a sneaky whisperer stealthily got inside my mind, controlling all my thoughts and feelings. The subtle message was to the effect that God loved me so much that He wanted to give me crystal clear evidence that my walk towards Christianity was a fake one. A vague hunch was hovering above the ceiling of my mind that Christianity was nothing but the path of the Devil; that's why God had removed all attacks against His Holy Qur'an, His Reverend Messenger and also removed all the poisons of the Bible. The premonition went on to say, "Now you have an unmistakable proof that you walked in the sidetrack of Christianity and deviated from the Truth. Arise now and repent. Do not tarry to ask the forgiveness of God since He is the oft-forgiver and Merciful to all those who repent and do well. Stand up and cleanse yourself from all the unclean thoughts coming from the Devil, defiling you and alluring you towards polytheism, blasphemy and infidelity." I could not help but to surrender to the Devil's admonitions.

When my Christian friend knew that I had lost all the papers, he was scared to death. He asked me not to see or contact him till we could see the result of losing those papers. This was the last straw I was clutching at and now I had lost all sources of support for continuing my walk in Christianity. So I felt as if God wanted me to abandon that religion, since I was unable to continue that battle. Although I enjoyed from the bottom of my heart and the depths of my soul every word of the Bible and did my best to keep saying the Lord's Prayer diligently, nothing was genuinely changed in my character. I was still full of hatred and envy towards Christians. I could not forgive anybody. I could not even say "Good morning" to my mother. I used to get out of my house with traces of anger, hatred and hostility painted on my face. I deliberately used to show anger toward my parents and brothers that they might know that they were infidels and that I hated them for that reason. I was so filled with the spirit of rebellion and hostility that I even doubted the authenticity of what I read in the Bible.

All those factors came together with the losing of the papers; it was a merciless attack to hinder the work of God in my life, an attempt to break my determination and my increasing love of the Bible. Once again, I broke into tears, blaming God for all my circumstances. I began to wonder if it was only God's doing that whenever I took a step towards Him things would go wrong.

"Why, Lord, do all these things happen to me? Why me? What did I do to deserve all that? If you are punishing me for something wrong I did to Christians, please forgive me now as I repent before you. Please have mercy upon me based on your death on the cross for me, or else your cross is nothing but what we used to think of it. Who are you that you would allow such a person like me to approach you? What can I do to please you? My life has become so miserable. If it continues like that, death will be easier for me than to continue to live as I am. Please God take my soul. If you don't have mercy on me, I will commit suicide. It will be no more harm to go to hell for that for if you don't bestow your mercy upon me, I will go to hell anyway."

I wept so much. I was wallowing in pain and agony. I stood up, with my tears running on my face like rivers. My mother saw me and patted my shoulders, and she cried with me. She asked me what was wrong with me. I told her, "Just leave me alone. I do not want to speak with anybody. I have once talked to you and you accused me of insanity. May God forgive you." I went quickly to my room and took a shower to cleanse my body from all the uncleanness of Christian thoughts. I also needed to wash myself from all I had done.

I kept on thinking, contemplating whether God would forgive me for all that I said regarding His Prophet Mohammad and His Holy Qur'an. I felt as if somebody was speaking to me saying, "You did not attack anybody or speak any kind of falsehood. All the conclusions that you reached was not of your manufacturing; they were self-evident." I stood up; spread, my prayer carpet, and

I repeated the two Islamic Testimonies in order to go back to Islam. I tried to pray unsuccessfully. I could not utter a word from the Qur'an. I could not bow down either. So, I placed my head between my palms for a while. Then I went away saying just few words, "Oh Lord, if you are not angry with me, nothing will do me any harm. If you are punishing me now for some transgression I did, I ask you to forgive me and ease my punishment. If you are standing against my help, that is foreign to your nature. Oh Lord, I have no more power to deal with my situation. If you will not reveal yourself to me, I will go astray. I love you Lord. I did what I was ordered to do. I did what all the others could not, just to please you, as I thought. When you revealed to me your light and called me, I did not delay. How long will you leave me groping in pitch darkness? All that is taking place in my life is a test of love you have prepared for me to lead me to your side. You are the Good Shepherd. Please give me more of your love and guidance to bring me more towards meeting you."

That night, I slept so deeply, like never before in all my life. When it was nearly dawn, I saw a vision while asleep. There was a hulk of a man with wide shoulders, a thick beard, bronze-colored face, long hair and a very beautiful complexion. He held me at my shoulders and shook me gently saying, "Do you still have doubts about me?" I told him, "Who are you that I have doubts in you? I don't know you." He said, "I am He for whom you are searching." I said, "No, please remind my failing memory." He said, "Read in the Book. Why didn't you read the Book?" I said, "Don't you know that I have lost the Book and all my papers, so how can I read now?" He said, "The Book cannot be lost. Stand up and open your closet and you will find it there; and all other papers will come back to you within a week."

I shuddered as if awakened by a whiplash and I went quickly to the small closet in one of the corners of my room. I was shivering when I opened it and to my great surprise, there I found the very book I had lost. I froze for a moment. I was shivering as if it was a chilly night in winter. I hugged the Bible tightly in my arms as a child who returned to his mother after a long time.

I ran to my mother, waking her up and smothering her with kisses. I told her with a great joy what happened that morning. I said, "I will never allow you to call me crazy any more." I threw myself into her arms, crying and saying, "Forgive me Mom, for treating you harshly. I thought that was according to the true faith. But now I know what the true faith is. Please, let me kiss your feet and I will not accept anything less."

She said, "Tell me my son, what happened to you?"

I answered, "I will tell you, but please swear to me by all that is dear to you, not to think that I have gone mad. My mother, God has guided me."

She asked, "And where have you been before?"

I replied, "God who guided me is not the one I was following before."

She responded, "Is there another God?"

I said, "Yes, there is another God who instructs me to love you and to obey you."

She asked, "Who is that God?"

I told her, "The Christ, Isa as the Qur'an says."

She urged me, "Please my son, don't say so before your brothers. They will think that you are really mad."

I said, "Ok, I will do as you say, but do you believe me?"

She looked at me and said, "Why wouldn't I believe you. I have already seen the evidence; you have never treated me like this in twenty years. Go, and God will never forsake you. But keep the matter a secret."

I confided, "Put yourself in my shoes, and you will understand my true feelings. I wish I could stand in a public place and shout at the top of my voice proclaiming that Christ is God and He has changed me. He did what the God of Mohammad was unable to do." She put her hand on my mouth to prevent me from speaking.

From that time, at the break of dawn and the rising of the sun, I would go out to people as if I were a newborn babe, seeing life for the first time. I went out early in the morning, looking at everything around me. I was able to see everything covered with beauty. All people were good in my eyes. I started to shake hands with all the people that I met, whether I knew them or not. I went to the Christian grocer. I used to harass him so much and when he saw me, he thought that I was coming to attack him. He started quickly to close his grocery. I called to him, "Don't be afraid." He was bewildered and uttered nothing. I hugged him and asked him to forgive me. He couldn't help but to cry. He said some words, I couldn't understand at the moment. Only later, I realized their full meaning. He said, "Hallelujah, Praise the Lord." I said, "What did you just say?" He said, "In His time, you will know what it means." After that, he went away.

I saw people from a new perspective. I wondered if I might have lost my sanity. People stared at me and wondered what had happened to me. Even my fellow workers were amazed at the sudden and radical change of my behavior. I could read astonishment on their faces saying, "This man used to spit on us yesterday. Now look at him; he is like a gentle lamb! What is going on? Is it a new tactic or plan against us?" I saw perplexity and confusion reflected on their faces, their high brows and wide-open eyes. They could not believe that my behavior could be changed 180 degrees. I didn't give much attention to their reactions. All that I cared about was to compensate those whom I had attacked, humiliated and insulted. I was beside myself with a joy that filled my heart. Meekness and calmness filled the inner curves of my innermost being for the first time in my whole life. I really thought that I was in a beautiful dream that I didn't want to wake up from. It was the power of God. I was in a hurry to get more of the experiences that would prove that I was really changed forever, not just temporarily.

I kept thinking about what the man I saw in my vision had said – I would find the papers within a week. Days went by and I began to doubt that vision. I was afraid that I might not find my papers and that probably would ruin my happiness. I kept on counting the days till there was one day left before the deadline given in the vision. On that day, I was near the train station and I wanted to make a phone call, so I had to go to the same phone booth where I had lost my papers a week ago. I hesitated for some time. I would go forward and then shrink back. The owner of the booth noted this, so he said to me, "I see you are in hesitation. Do you have a problem?" I said, "No, this phone is a bad omen for me since I used it last week and I lost my bag. I don't want to use it again since I don't know what am I going to lose." He inquired, "Was it your bag?" I answered, " Yes, do you know where it is?" He responded, "Give me some description of the bag to show me that it really belongs to you and I will tell you where it is." I told him that it was a plastic bag with some papers, a Book like the Qur'an, my ID, and my passport. There was no money in the bag. He nodded and said, "That's correct." He told me to come the following day and he would take me to the one who found it.

The following day was the seventh day since I had seen the vision. We went to a village in the suburbs of Cairo towards the south. We met the man who found the bag. He gave it back to me. I quickly opened it but I did not find the book. I said to him, "There is a book missing." He said, "I swear by the Name of God, I did not take anything from the bag. It includes papers, passport, ID, and a Qur'an (Holy Bible)." I was glad to hear that and I told him that I really believed him. That meant that God had fulfilled His promise to me that He gave me back the very lost Book.

I was on cloud nine; in all my Islamic life, I had never experienced asking something from God and receiving an answer. This was a super miracle for me. I felt so small and humble before the grace of God. I said to God, "Who am I that you would give me all these favors?" Soon the answer came to me, "I did so and I will continue to do greater things for those who love God." I was talking to myself, wishing that God would let me go through an experience that would make me quite certain that I was really changed. That would really make me glad.

Soon God answered my prayers. He gave me my first experience in my new relationship with Christ. At my job, employees used to receive periodical financial awards, each one in his turn. I would bully the payroll personnel, forcing them to place me at the top of the list. I also used to take a percentage of all those awards because the money belonged to Christian infidels; therefore it should not be distributed equally.

One day, it was time to receive the money from the company's cashier. One of my colleagues had very hard circumstances at home; so he came to the manager and begged him to give the money to him this time so that he could get out of the financial dilemma. The manager told him that the list was already arranged and everyone had his turn. The manager said to him, "Mr. X is on the top of the list and you know that he is an evil man and we cannot let him wait. We have to please him by any means to fend off his evil." At this moment, I entered the office of the manager to find him whispering with my colleague. I asked them quickly, "Are you speaking about the award?" The manager answered in a manner tinted with awkwardness and clumsiness: "Yes, but don't worry. Your name is on top of the list." I asked him, "So what does my colleague want?" He replied, "He wants to have his turn this month to get out of his financial difficulty, but I refused his request." I asked, "Why? You can put his name instead of mine." The manager thought that I was making fun of him. He said, "Your name is on top of the list and nobody can remove it." I said, "But I want to give it up to him this month." He said, "That's impossible. You…You can do so?" I said, "Yes." He wondered, "How?" I answered, "I'm telling you; please remove my name and put him in my place. It is better that all of our colleagues will also give up their turns for him." I heard him saying, "Glory be to God who can change circumstances. What is going on? What has happened? Maybe it is Doomsday today! That person could do so! I can't believe it!" I said, "God is Omnipotent and He can get 'Out of the eater, something to eat; and out of the strong, something sweet.'" My eyes were wet with tears in that situation, which was the first of its kind in my whole life. I used to take the lion's share of everything, legally or illegally. But now Christ has taught me how to give. I was thrilled to enjoy the ecstatic taste of giving.

My family began to feel the change in my life. They used to turn off the TV and run away as soon as they caught sight of me, especially my sisters. After that day of transformation, I would enter our house and let them watch TV. I just asked them to avoid the indecent programs. They said, "That's impossible. You allow us to watch TV? No way!" I answered, "Why not? If you knew what I feel for you, you would not believe how much I love you. I want you to forgive me for all my misbehavior towards you." Immediately, all of them burst into tears. Whenever I would go out, upon my return I would kiss my mother, bringing her a present every now and then. She would cry. I am thankful to God that when she died we were on good terms and I managed to make amends for what I had done to her. I was very grateful to that God who returned the smile to all our family members, believers and non-believers.

My Christian friends were following all the events that took place and were afraid that people of the village would discover my situation and then it would recoil upon their heads since they were my friends. So they asked me to leave Egypt and travel abroad, but I refused categorically. I was still aware of what I had done against Christ and the Christians. Therefore, I told them I had prayed from the first day my life was changed that God would help me to serve Christ as much as I opposed Him. I had persecuted His people in Egypt so I would not leave Egypt. I promised them that I would not mention their names anyway if I were arrested. One day, they asked me to go to a church I had never visited before and I agreed. I met some of the fathers and I told them all that God had done with me. Their faces were lit up with pleasure and they were thrilled for the great wonders God did in my life. I wanted to be baptized. They responded to my request. I was baptized on May 9th, 1993. I still remember that day since I consider it my real birthday. It is closely connected with the time I was born again.

FRUITS OF FAITH

I talked in detail about my life before my conversion. It is time now that I tell you about the work of God in my life after I came to know Him. All of my relatives, friends and acquaintances could not believe that I could change so radically. No one could believe what took place after my regeneration. Once I asked God to give me some experiences to prove to me that I was really converted. Actually God gave me lots of experiences, not only to prove the change to me, but also to train me for those soon to come hard and thorny challenges. I didn't choose the new way, not even my life with Christ. On the contrary, I tried to deny what I saw. It was Christ who chose me. He didn't choose me haphazardly but specifically for a purpose and ministry He had already prepared for me. I am sure He also prepared me for that kind of ministry. With this in mind, I would like to mention some of the dangerous experiences I faced and how God used me.

I used to work in an office with three other colleagues. We used to work in shifts so we rarely got together. Each of us had his own locker where we kept personal belongings. One day I was surprised to discover that some of my things were missing. I didn't suspect any of my colleagues. The next day, the same thing happened and I discovered the loss of more items. I actually blamed my wife, but when the same thing took place for the third time and my salary was stolen, I realized that the lock was broken. I knew that one of my colleagues was responsible. Suddenly a terrible Satanic Spirit of anger controlled me. I started to swear and curse in my old manner, just like I did before salvation. I said, "Now that I have accepted Christ and you have seen me meek like a lamb, you think you can make fun of me, well I'm not easy prey."

I swore to get even with them and pay them back double. I made up my mind to break all their lockers and take all their belongings and burn them. I will leave all the lockers open, like Abraham had done with the idols. I wanted them to know the feelings of those who got robbed and looted. I went and fetched a big hammer to carry out my plan. I closed the office and after making sure nobody was watching, I grabbed the hammer with both hands and swung it in the air. I was reeking with anger and shivering with a burning desire for revenge. I was about to hit the lockers when I felt something holding my hands and a gentle voice saying, "Do not repay evil with evil or insult with insult, but with blessing; be a peace maker." I turned around to see who was talking, but nobody was there. I said to myself, "Oh Lord, do you agree with what has happened to me? Your will be done. Please extinguish my fury and quench the fire of my wrath. I can hardly control myself. Please give me peace." Suddenly, I felt a strange peace surrounding me, as if nothing had happened. I heard a voice asking me to write on a paper the following:

"My dear brother who opens my locker,

I am sorry for not being able to meet your needs. Please write down all that you need and I, by the grace of God, will do my best to help you. To prove my good intention and honesty, I will not exchange the broken lock. I know that the love of God is exceeding great to all of us human beings. Finally, I hope that the peace of God that surpasses all minds will keep your life forever.

Your Brother"

After writing that letter I put it in my locker and left it as it was. I prayed and gave thanks to God for preventing me from being misguided by satanic thoughts. I went home and hugged my wife as soon as she opened the door. She said, "Don't be afraid. If God is with us who can be against us? As for the stolen money, the Bible says, "I was young and now I am old, yet I have never seen the righteous forsaken or their children begging bread." (PS 37:25) God can meet all our needs since He is our Provider."

Two days later we got a surprise. One of my colleagues came to the office during my shift. That was unusual. I asked him, "What brings you in at this time?" He said, "I'd like to talk to you." "What do you want to say?" I asked. He told me it was better to go to a quiet place to speak with each other. So we sat facing each other. He looked down and said, "I don't know what to say to you. I don't know what to do." I said, "Tell me what happened." He opened a small bag and showed me all the items he had taken from my locker. I couldn't believe my eyes. It did not occur to me that those things could ever be returned. I did not expect a man like him to be the thief. He was a religious man who used to keep prayers regularly. He said: "Those are the things I took from your locker; please take them back and don't tell anybody. As for the money, I cannot pay you back right now since my children have been so ill and I had to take them to the doctor. I can pay you back on a monthly basis." I said, "You can take all these things. They are yours now. I didn't lie when I wrote you the letter. God will compensate me for everything; you take the money. I am sure God will provide for everything. Had I been dishonest, I wouldn't have left my locker open with a broken lock."

He said, "I just have one question. I want you to answer me frankly." I responded, "Have I lied to you before?" He said, "No." I inquired, "What is your question?" He began, "You speak like Christians saying Lord, Lord. You use the same words and expressions that I often hear from Gergis the carpenter, my neighbor, who's a Christian." I said to him, "In fact, when I discovered that my items were stolen, I had two options, either to repay aggression with aggression, and tit for tat according to the Hadith that says, 'He who dies without his money, he is a martyr,' and 'None of you shall be a sissy, just take your due rights and pay attention to nothing else.' In other words, I have the option how I can get back my belongings.

The other option was not to repay evil with evil and not to avenge myself. If someone wants to sue me and take my tunic, I must let him have my cloak as well. Which of the two ways is better in your opinion?" He said, "The second option is much better, of course." I said, "That's what I did. I behaved in a way so as to keep the bonds of love and cordiality, disregarding the source of that pattern of behavior whether coming from Islam, Christianity or Judaism. What counts is the behavior itself. If I found such a behavior in Islam, for example, I would have behaved accordingly without hesitation." He wondered, "From where have you got this? Where have you learned these concepts?" I answered, "I will tell you later. Now you are tense. Some time later when you take some rest, I will share with you, maybe after a couple of days or a month. If you are still interested to know, I will never hesitate to tell you."

Two weeks later, after he finished his shift, my colleague came to me and said, "Now I have simmered down and I am still interested to know the source of your teachings, as you promised." I said to him, "I will see you tomorrow to tell you all that you want." The following day, he met with me and asked me the same question. I said to him, "One moment." I took the Bible out and said, "If you really want to know where I have learned all that, read this book." He said, "This is a Bible! God forbid!" I said, "Yes, this is the Bible and you are totally free to read it if you would like to know. You can take it if you want. If not, it is up to you." He took the Book and kept on turning it on both sides and looking at it in astonishment. Finally, he took it and left. I said, "If you encounter any difficulty, you can ask me."

For two weeks, he kept on coming to me with several questions. He continued to read the Bible till I noticed a big change in his life. His love of the Bible remarkably increased. One day, he said, "This book contains a great blessing. Since I started to read it, my relationship with my wife has gotten better and all our differences have vanished." I said, "Read more to know what you ought to do." He absorbed the Bible quickly.

One day, he came to me and suddenly asked me to teach him the Christian prayer. He wanted to know what it was like. I told him that it did not have a specific form. "You can pray in any position using any style," I said. After three months he came and it was a big surprise to see him hugging and embracing me warmly. He asked me how he could be baptized. My friend accepted the Lord and he was a tremendous blessing to his whole family. I was glad to feel that God had chosen me to work in His vineyard and to be one of His sheep. It was a privilege to be one of those who lead people, not to delusion and deception, but to Salvation and Eternal Life. In the past, I used to catch people to bring them to destruction. How wonderful to work with the Lord, the Rock of ages, the Savior Jesus Christ.

For the first time, I began to feel that I loved my country and my people. I started to love forgiveness and tolerance. I became a new creation. God used me to attract many souls to Christ, bringing back many sheep that had gone astray leaving Christ. I went through many experiences that detected the remaining parts of the old self in my nature. With the remaining parts of the old self came many attacks of Satan on my spirit and body as well.

One day, I went to visit my family. I took a minibus. I heard the driver calling the passengers to come and take their places inside the minibus, so I entered and the man let me sit on a chair that accommodated three passengers – but I was the fourth. Beside me, there was a heavy, bearded, strict, religious man and his veiled wife beside him. The man was unfriendly towards me. He looked at me and pressed me to a very narrow space. He stretched his legs, leaving me only a few inches of space. When I saw this, I left the car. The driver asked me what was wrong. I told him there was no place for me. He told me the seat is for four passengers and he asked the Sheikh to give me some space. But I felt that that man did not want any body to sit beside him so that no one would bother his wife. Consequently, I went out and paid for the fourth 'place' so that nobody would sit beside them. I asked the driver to give them the whole space so that no one would bother his wife. The man noticed this, and with that, his manhood, chivalry and courtesy were suddenly awakened in him. He insisted that I sit beside him. I told him there was no need that I would squash them, but he insisted that I sit with them. He gave me enough space.

The minibus moved for some meters and the man asked me an unexpected question, "Are you Moslem or a Christian?" I asked him, "Why do you want to know?" He said, "I just want to know." I said, "I am a Christian." He lamented, "Alas, were you a Moslem, this behavior of yours would have been more significant." I asked, "Do you know me?" He said, "No." I pointed out, "Neither do I know you. But why do you think I would do this for you?" He replied, "Well, I don't know." I told him that we have a text in the Bible that admonishes us to love all people, including those who hurt us.

"I noticed how harsh you had been with me and I just wanted to show you that type of love that fills us towards all who hate us." He then asked, "Do you have a book?" I answered, "Yes." He asked, "Do you worship God?" I said, "Who else can we worship?" He said, "I know that you worship Christ, priests and monks, as the Qur'an said." I said, "Not all that you know about us is correct. Otherwise you wouldn't have admired my behavior towards you. I suggest something." He said, "Yes?" I gave him a Bible and said to him, "This book includes the Old and New Testaments. Read it and see what is inside. If you like it, good; if not, you have nothing to lose." I gave him the Bible and we agreed to meet somewhere later.

We used to meet every week to discuss his questions. After that we began to pray together. He started to have some arguments with his wife and he wanted to divorce her. I told him that divorce was against the will of God. We prayed for his wife and his family sustained peace and closeness. I told him that Christianity was a type of life that gathered – instead of scattering – people, and quoted to him, "The unbelieving husband is sanctified in his believing wife and vice versa." My friend was euphoric about the teachings of the Bible. The Lord entered his house and brought solidity, peace and blessing.

I don't want to finish my testimony. Actually, it is an on-going testimony. As long as the Lord is working in me the testimony continues.

To sum up I want to say that God has given me this life for free. If we consider any other options, we will find nothing but destruction, devastation and sin. God does not mention our sins anymore. We enjoy freedom since the Son has set us free and we have become free indeed. Life is Christ and death is gain. I am filled with that feeling for the first time in my whole life. In the past, death was an ugly and fearful ghost. I was afraid of the torture of the grave and the questioning of the two angels, etc. Now I say good-bye to you, my dear reader, till we meet in a new thrilling experience of the endless precious divine dealings of the Lord who is able to guard what has been entrusted to Him.

Yours,

Paul

I Was Dead and Now I Live

I am the seventh of fourteen children. We live in one of the poor, densely populated areas, where Muslims and Christians live together. I grew up in a Muslim family. My father worked hard to make ends meet. He worked day and night to earn our living. My brothers and me used to spend most of our time hanging around on the streets. Hunger would motivate us to steal loaves of bread or some bottles of milk that had been left early in the morning in front of the not-yet-opened shops.

As a child, I was not fond of education and before long I was kicked out of school. I still remember that there was a pious Christian lady that used to gather the children off the street to give them Sunday school lessons. She used to teach us about the love of Jesus Christ to all people, show us spiritual films and read us some passages from the Bible. At the end of the meeting, she gave us some candy and drinks. She treated us kindly and gently; therefore, we would feel ashamed of ourselves had we had harmed her in any way!

There were no activities for children provided by cultural institutions or clubs, only that loving lady. As a boy, I enjoyed the Christian festivals on Christmas and Easter. They were joyful occasions for me.

After being kicked out of school I started to work as a laborer in the seaport and other places. I was living in a big vacuum, a terrible vacuum. I was lonely with no friend or companion to care for me. I was brought up in a family with one foundation – the love of money. I was materialistic. I was enslaved by money.

Being kicked out of school had a negative effect on me. I took refuge in alcohol to forget my problems. I tried to find solutions in gambling and drinking. I saw life in terms of having fun and collecting money. My brothers joined the trades and started to make good money. I was green with envy and I decided to start my own business. I managed to open a small shop and actually started to make some money, but no peace or tranquility!

I didn't have inner peace. I always felt deadly emptiness. This lasted for six years. Family problems began to surface. My brothers and sisters had marital problems, my father grew old, and my mother fell ill. All the problems rested upon my shoulders. In 1982, I was up to my ears in debts. All the constant pressures of various problems resulted in a severe depression. Finally I collapsed in 1986.

Looking back at my life before the collapse, I was an alcoholic. Between 1982 and 1984, I used to drink heavily and frantically. In 1984, I traveled to France to get treatment from severe psychological problems. I was treated for one month and then I went back home. I was shocked to find the shop and the business I had established completely demolished.

In August 1986, I began to feel a terrible pain in my stomach and some other parts of my body. I was hospitalized in a coma. I was in a serious condition. The mechanism in my body nearly stopped. For 17 days, my friends and relatives came to visit me in the hospital. They expected me to die soon. One of them was a Christian clergyman. I still remember him for his love and humility. Some other Christian friends also visited me and prayed for me.

At this time, the nurses went on a strike in my hospital and they had to get rid of the patients who were not seriously ill. I remained in the hospital. After 17 days of my medical treatment, I became hysterical. I jumped out of my bed and attacked all those around me, and I cut the oxygen tubes; soon I lost consciousness. Physicians thought that my end was coming. Doctors examined me and after an hour they decided that I was dead!!! They called my family to come in order to issue my death certificate. While I was in that condition, I saw an intense light touching me, and I heard a voice three times saying, "Stand up!" I saw the person of Jesus Christ. He appeared to me through that great light.

My family brought a casket to take my dead body from the hospital. However, after Jesus appeared to me, I I recovered.

When doctors came to me and saw me, they were shocked. They wrote a medical report and described my case as "a very rare, freak, inexplicable case!!!" I am sure it was Jesus Christ who brought me back to life. He said, "I am the way and the truth and the life." (John 14:6)

I left the hospital in a feeble condition, but I was newly born, for I came to believe in Jesus Christ as my Savior. I told him, "Lord, if you want to give me life, let it be for the glory of your name." I became, once again, childlike. I began to see everything from a new viewpoint. I wanted to be with Christian brothers. When I walked on the street, people would point at me and say, "He was dead but now he lives."

In fact, the Lord Jesus has changed my life. One day I was walking and I passed by a bookstore. After some hesitation, I knocked. A gentle lady opened the door and welcomed me in. Among other books I saw a Bible. I remembered the Christian lady who used to teach us at Sunday School Classes when I was a boy. I thought this lady might know something about her, so I asked her. She said, "Of course I know her; she is in a seniors' nursing home, but maybe she is dead by now."

I decided to visit her the following day. I entered the place to see a woman sleeping on a chair. I remembered the songs of Sunday school, and I started to sing. She opened her eyes and asked, "Who are you?" I said, "I am Sayed. Do you remember me? It was 35 years ago." I told her my story and how I became a Christian. She said, "Great, but be careful, Sayed. Be faithful in your life with the Lord!"

I started my walk by putting my faith in Jesus Christ. I started to read the Bible and experience real life with the Lord. I was so thirsty. I used to read to quench my thirst with the Word of Life. With all my weaknesses and shortcomings, I could see the Lord restoring me. It was God who gave us the promise, "And surely I am with you always, to the very end of the age" (Matt. 28:20). He also said: "I am the light of the world. Whoever follows me will never walk in darkness, but will have the light of life." (John 8:12)

Experiential fellowship with God is really great. Whenever I sought God, I had an unimaginable inner peace filling my innermost being. I can really identify with the father who said about his prodigal son, "For this son of mine was dead and is alive again; he was lost and is found.' So they began to celebrate." (Luke 15:32) I once was dead, but now I am alive; I once was lost, but now I am found.

IMPORTANT
INSTRUCTIONS

My dear Brothers and Sisters,

What you have just read is not fiction woven by our imagination. It is reality. We lived these facts; these are our lives. We don't speak about a Christ that we do not know, but we have spoken of what we saw with our own eyes… touched with our hands… realized by our minds… comprehended in our hearts.

Since we live in a country that does not give any freedom of faith in our Lord and Savior Jesus Christ, we are unable to publish our names, addresses and photos. However, let all people know that in those countries that blaspheme against Christ by refusing to recognize Him as Lord and God, thousands of knees shall bow, worship and live for Jesus Christ.

Faith in Jesus Christ as Lord and Savior is neither impossible nor as difficult as you may imagine. You just need to:

- Believe that Jesus Christ is God and Savior since He is the only Way, Truth and Life. There is no one but Him and no other gods.

- Proclaim your repentance for all your sins, selfishness and all those things that have hindered your mature human walk.

- Make a free decision to live for Him completely, allowing Him to sanctify you by regenerating the intentions of your heart and behavior. He will make of you a light in darkness, and you will become the salt of the earth.

My dear brother and sister, I want you to know that our Lord and Savior Jesus Christ is not forcing us to follow Him as slaves. He doesn't want us to proclaim our faith in public squares or street corners. He doesn't want us to fast and change our faces to be known to all people as people who fast. Our Lord and Savior Jesus Christ is against all sorts of pride, deceit, fake mannerisms or hypocrisy. He is the God who sees the secret desires of the heart and the inner true reality of your self. He requests that your faith be from the heart and that you fast and pray secretly. Your relationship with Him is a personal fellowship and it is far from being just a hollow fake motto.

"What good will it be for a man if he gains the whole world and loses his soul." (Matt. 16:26)

"Ask and it will be given to you; seek and you will find; knock and the door will be opened to you. For everyone who asks receives; he who seeks finds; and to him who knocks, the door will be opened. (Mat 7:7)